Charlie.
May you Guide
your clients to S
& Success! J

Praise for Jason Cutter and
Selling With Authentic Persuasion

"No matter what you think your job or role is...You are in Sales. Period. We can all benefit from Jason's learned wisdom on how to authentically influence others."

— Rylee Meek, Founder of Social Dynamic Selling

"Most people see 'selling' as something really negative. However, the best salespeople are those committed to getting clients what they truly need. Jason's book gives a blueprint to be successful in sales, and in life, by being authentic and honest."

— Jamie Sarche, Director of Preplanning, Feldman Mortuary

"This is not your typical sales book. In fact, arguably it's more about relationships than sales. And that is what is so refreshing about Jason's approach. He recognizes that getting someone to buy is not mechanical, but rather more emotional. It's about how they come to know you, like you, and trust you."

— Frank Agin, President, AmSpirit Business Connections

"When I began reading *Selling With Authentic Persuasion*, I found this passage, which sets the stage for any person wanting to become a sales professional. 'The point of the sales professional is to help people achieve their goals, avoid pain, and fundamentally, end up in a better place as a result of dealing with us.' Exactly, Jason! Bravo!"

— Ken Lazar, CEO and Professional Sales Recruiter

"As a solopreneur, this book was a gold mine for me. I'm someone who resists being a 'salesman,' but Jason does a great job of describing the power of this approach. After realizing the error in my approach (being an order taker), I will be adjusting immediately."

— Kyle Gillette, Creator of the SAGE Mindset Framework

"Jason Cutter does a fantastic job of walking you through the process of finding who you are as a salesperson and focusing on your strengths. If you are looking for a great way to move your sales performance ahead and want to really help your prospects, you should invest in this book."

— Ian Peterman, CEO, Peterman Design Firm

"In a culture that teaches you how to pretend and manipulate, this book very clearly states how being authentic is the actual key to sales success. Highly recommended for anyone in sales at any stage of their career."

— Donald Meador, Author of *Surrounded by Insanity: How to Execute Bad Decisions*

"Whether you're just setting out on a career as a seller or have been in the game for years, Jason's perspective on authenticity and mindset and his roadmap for succeeding in the profession of sales are not to be missed!"

— Catie Ivey, RVP of Sales, Demandbase

"Jason is an incredible thought leader in the field of sales. His unique approach builds on who you are as a person to leverage authenticity for maximum persuasion. I highly recommend this book to anyone who is looking to get an edge without sacrificing who they are at their core."

— Kwame Christian, Esq., MA, Director of the
American Negotiation Institute

"Every person in sales *must read* this incredibly inspirational book. Sales is more an art than a science, and art is about being authentic. If you believe in being better, then this approach is what you need."

— John Waid, CEO & Author of *ReInventing Ralph: A Little Story for Salespeople About Culture-Driven Selling*

"Step by step, Jason Cutter shows you how to elevate selling into a calling by applying your authentic self, signature strengths, and leadership skills to create lasting value for your customers and clients."

— Wayne Baker, Author of *All You Have to Do Is Ask*,
Professor of Business Administration at the University
of Michigan Ross School of Business

"For me, it's all about the title. Being Authentic is sometimes hard to achieve when you are in the selling mode; however, after reading this book, being authentic will become second nature. Jason takes you step-by-step and helps you self-identify your authenticity. Once you do that, all other things fall into place. Great read and can't wait to share with my team."

— Jamey Vumback, CEO/Founder GetTheReferral.com

"Early in my career, I heard a truth described this way: 'If you can see through John Brown's eyes, you can sell John Brown the way John Brown buys.' Jason Cutter's book provides many things with one of the best being *how* to see through your customer's eyes."

— Bob Sager, Author of *101 Freaking Brilliant Business Ideas: And Ten Ways YOU Can Create Your Own*

"*Selling With Authentic Persuasion* taught me to sell like a doctor. Its many stories contain nuggets of wisdom I will use in my sales career, both for myself and for my clients. I am glad Jason explored these topics, and in so doing so, taught me to sell like a professional."

— Alex Pop, Writer

"The essence of sales is highlighting to a prospect/customer a ROI (return on investment) for the product or service you are selling; i.e., Will the dollar I spend provide me with more value than the cost itself? Keeping that in mind, after reading *Selling With Authentic Persuasion*, you should receive a multiple ROI."

— Adam Connors, Founder, NetWorkwise

"If you learn one thing today, I hope it is that everyone is a salesperson. Whether you're selling a product or a service, asking for a raise or trying to get your kids to do what you want them to, you sell. It is a skill you can learn, and to get started, you must read this book. It really gets to the point in helping you learn to sell, but in a way that you will feel comfortable. Great job, Jason Cutter."

— Danny P. Creed, Global Business Coach, Speaker, Trainer, and Sales Expert

"'Prescription before diagnosis is malpractice.' This statement applies to doctors as it does to salespeople. Jason Cutter hits a home run with this comprehensive book on the psychology of sales from the perspective of the ego. Both salesperson and prospect have fears, and Jason shows how to become aware of them and use that understanding to develop empathy to consistently achieve the best outcome in any sales interaction. Hands-on and written with personal anecdotes and case studies, this is the most comprehensive primer on sales I have ever read."

— Eli Angote, Founder at TheBestNotary.net

"If authenticity is the key, then Jason is walking the talk in this book. Not only do I agree with the methods he purports as a way to bust quotas, but his style of writing is also a lesson for readers—if nothing else, authentically mimic his authenticity and you will find increased success!"

— Bill Eckstrom, CEO, EcSell Institute

"Authenticity is the road to trust. One must be honest with themselves in order for others to trust them. When the trust is built, then you can facilitate a transformation in your prospect's life, big or small, through what you are selling—whether it is a product, service, or idea."

— Rob Howze, Empowerment Artist and founder of World Wide Community

"*Selling With Authentic Persuasion* is the book you need not only to sell, but to feel good about your sales career. Jason Cutter provides invaluable tools so you can learn to sell in honest, helpful ways that will have customers trusting you enough to keep coming back. It's a tour-de-force that will revolutionize the sales industry."

— Patrick Snow, Publishing Coach and International Best-Selling Author of *Creating Your Own Destiny* and *Boy Entrepreneur*

"In *Selling With Authentic Persuasion*, Jason Cutter reveals how you can sell with truth and integrity. He analyzes the fear of being seen as a dishonest or pushy salesperson, which lies at the heart of most salespeople's problems, and he shows how you can remain authentic to both yourself and those who buy from you so everyone feels good."

— Nicole Gabriel, Author of *Finding Your Inner Truth* and *Stepping Into Your Becoming*

"I love how Jason Cutter presents the primary problem with customer service today—the fear that being a salesperson is a bad thing. In *Selling With Authentic Persuasion*, he shows how you can go from order taker to quota breaker through honesty, listening, and serving the customer. I wish I'd had this book when I managed a customer service department. It's invaluable."

— Tyler R. Tichelaar, PhD and Award-Winning Author of *When Teddy Came to Town*

SELLING WITH AUTHENTIC PERSUASION

TRANSFORM FROM ORDER TAKER TO QUOTA BREAKER

JASON CUTTER

AVIVA
PUBLISHING
New York

SELLING WITH AUTHENTIC PERSUASION:
TRANSFORM FROM ORDER TAKER TO QUOTA BREAKER

Published by:
Aviva Publishing
Lake Placid, NY
(518) 523-1320
www.AvivaPublishing

Jason Cutter
(206) 234-1848
Jason@AuthenticPersuasion.com
www.AuthenticPersuasion.com

ISBN: 9781890427375
Library of Congress: 2020911330

Editors: Larry Alexander and Tyler Tichelaar, Superior Book
Productions
Cover Design and Interior Book Layout: Nicole Gabriel, Angel
Dog Productions
Author Photo: Rob Arnold

Every attempt has been made to properly source all quotes.

Printed in the United States of America

To my parents, Mike and Norma

No matter what choices I made or where my winding path took me, their unconditional love and support have been the one consistent part of my life. Without it, I don't know if I would have taken the indirect path in life that led me to discovering who I truly am.

ACKNOWLEDGMENTS

Writing a book is the final manifestation of a long journey in which many people have played their parts to make it happen. I want to thank my biggest cheerleaders who have always been there for me—my parents. I know at times in my adult life they were concerned with my choices that were outside of a stable, regular paycheck and benefits path, but they never told me I was doing the wrong thing. They let me live my life with unconditional love and support. That is all a son could ever ask for.

I am eternally thankful to have had an amazing grandma, Helen, who was always the voice of faith in there being a plan with things that happen in life. While she is no longer with us, her voice still plays in my mind telling me I deserve to be happy, shouldn't put up with any crap, and that "God don't make junk." She never saw anything but greatness in me.

I know I would also not be the man I am today without the influence and support of my papa, Norm. His strengths were fortunately passed down to my mom, then down to me. He has always been a stable rock.

If you have never written a book before, it's not a simple process. For me it was full of excitement, doubt, struggles, and breakthroughs. I write like I speak, never did well in grammar—was more of a math and science person. I want to thank Tyler Tichelaar for molding my raw text and into something very precious. As you read through this, feeling it is concise and well structured—that was Tyler's expert editorial craftsmanship.

I had a plan to write a book, even started one ten years ago, and felt the best person to help me achieve this undertaking was Patrick Snow. I am so glad I met him in Seattle in 2009 at a networking event, and since then, he has become my guide on this journey. I appreciate his patience with me as I wrote out the first version, then literally threw it away and stopped working on it for months. His faith that I had a great message inside of me and that he knew how to make it a reality is why you are reading this book.

While I had all the parts of the book in place based on how I had helped countless salespeople, I was not clear on my overall message. It wasn't until I started working with the amazing Sam Crowley that I was able to get clear on my message and the value of my story as a way to inspire and teach others. The theme of helping people *Transform from Order Taker to Quota Breaker* was the result of his dissection of what made me tick.

There is one group of people I must thank, but there is no way I could list them all—the prospects I have spoken with, the ones who have trusted me enough to buy, and the ones who didn't. Truly none of this book would have been possible without all those conversations and experiences; specific ones are still in my mind, some of which took place seventeen years ago. They all left their own impressions on me and allowed me to shape my sales process into the Authentic Persuasion method. If you are one of them, I may never speak with you again so I cannot thank you in person, but I hope you enjoyed the sales experience as much as I did and are still happy with your purchase.

Lastly, I would be remiss if I didn't acknowledge the biggest provider of opportunities for growth and discovery in my life. While at times I wasn't happy with you, in retrospect I can see you just wanted me to become the type of person who could inspire others to transform into the most authentic versions of themselves. We have had our ups and downs—some really wonderful experiences and some tragic punches in the face that I wouldn't wish on anyone else. Through it all, as long as I didn't stop, I kept faith that you would have something better for me at some point. Everything happens for a reason, and I wouldn't want to go back and change anything because it has all given me a lot of "character." For that, I thank you, LIFE.

CONTENTS

PREFACE

"Try not. Do...or do not. There is no try."

— Yoda

Before you decide to buy this book or invest your time in reading it, I want to make sure it will be the right investment for you.

This might seem like an odd statement to begin a book, but if you have just picked up this book and plan to skim through it to determine if you want to buy it, hopefully, you will start here. Most authors are in the business of writing books as a source of income and to build prestige. But this author wants to make sure this book is worth your time and money.

As you will discover on our journey together, I am a bit different in my philosophies. My goal is to help salespeople go from being order takers to quota breakers and, ultimately, to becoming sales superstars who will create lives of freedom for themselves. The method to get there is Authentic Persuasion. It is the same sales method I use, so it only makes sense that this book would be written the same way.

This book IS NOT for you, if:

- You feel like you have been doing sales long enough that you already know it all.

- You don't think anyone could teach you anything new about sales.

- You say things like "That's not how we did it at our last company" or "This is how I have always done it."

- You are happy with your level of success in sales.

- You do not want to be a sales superstar (because you know it will take effort, focus, and time you do not want to invest).
- You read books designed to provide both insight and useful ways to improve some aspect of your life, yet never put into place anything you read, and maybe even blame the author for wasting your time.

If you find yourself identifying with this list of reasons, then I appreciate your level of self-awareness. Of course, if you don't buy this book, I will never know you were on that list (unless you want to email me at jason@authenticpersuasion.com). Even if we never cross paths, it still makes me happy to know you made a decision that was authentic and true for yourself, and saved some time and effort. .

This book IS for you, if:

- You are an experienced, veteran salesperson who has hit a plateau or lost your mojo.
- You are a new salesperson who has yet to create consistent success.
- You are thinking about getting into a sales role but aren't sure if you really have what it takes to succeed.
- You are open to learning new subjects.
- You are willing to be honest with yourself regarding your strengths and weaknesses.
- You are coachable and have the desire to change aspects that might not be working in your sales career and life.
- You have a sales process developed by your company (maybe even required) and you know there are always new ways to add to or complement that process to close more sales.
- You don't have a sales process, your company hasn't provided you much scripting or training, and you want any help you can get.

- You recognize you might be an order taker, but you have the desire to be successful in sales.

- You don't know if you want to be in sales, or if sales is the right fit for you, but you are willing to figure it out.

- You know a sales career could lead to an amazing level of financial freedom.

- You know a salesperson's skills cannot be taken away and can be used in any part of the world.

If you identify with the list of reasons to read this book, then let's start this journey together! I am excited you are here because it means you are looking for some gems of knowledge to get you to the next level in your sales career, whether that's sales superstar status or going from order taker to quota breaker. Be assured you've now found that gem, and its name is Authentic Persuasion

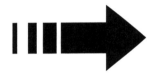

TAKING CHARGE OF YOUR SALES CAREER

"Sales are contingent upon the attitude of the salesman, not the attitude of the prospect."

— William Clement Stone

You found yourself in a sales job, but you just can't seem to be successful. Other reps around you close deals with ease—blowing past the quota and earning bonuses—yet you struggle even to close the minimum number of sales.

It feels like you can never win—people don't buy from you on the spot, and none of your follow-up calls lead to anything. Even when you have a good week, the next one is usually a complete letdown. As you go to bed each night, you wonder if you should change careers. Each week ends leaving you unsure if you want to go back on Monday. Maybe you wonder if you will even have a job to go back to.

Are you questioning your decision to become a sales professional? Do you wonder how you got into this role and if you are really meant to be in sales? Are you living paycheck to paycheck because you can barely make quota? If you do have a good week or month, do you find it doesn't happen twice in a row, making you feel like sales are all about luck? Deep down inside, do you like the idea of helping people, but you would never want to force someone to buy from you?

I know your pain. Early in my sales career, I was in that same spot. I didn't want to be that pushy, manipulative salesperson I was warned about when I was growing up, but I found myself in a sales role without any real guidance or training. During my career, I have also seen that same scenario play out with countless reps who had great intentions, but at the end of the day, weren't provided proper selling tools, so they ultimately failed to be successful and moved on to new careers.

This book was designed to be the roadmap to fill in the missing pieces of your sales success and has been separated into three sections. In Section 1, you will uncover a formula for creating an authentic you that will facilitate your sales success. Together, we will look at how your fears affect interactions with prospects, and you will uncover the power of embracing your strengths instead of worrying about your weaknesses. You will come to understand that being a sales professional is actually about developing the leadership skills to move your prospects past their own fears.

In Section 2, we will focus on the persuasion part of the equation. I will show you what a successful salesperson looks like. (Hint: It has nothing to do with classic sales tactics.) Then we will dive into sales fundamentals and explore ways that building rapport, asking questions, having empathy for your prospects, and moving conversations forward like a doctor does with their patients will lead you to sales success.

In Section 3, I will share with you the intangibles of a success sales career. Intangibles are those small, hard to track, sometimes difficult to "put your finger on" ways that create a higher level of effectiveness. When you start to master the reasons you get in your own way with prospects, learn to avoid the reasons so many salespeople struggle with their pipeline, and help your prospects move forward with buying from you while at the same time mitigating their buyer's remorse, you will create consistent and greater results. The last part is tying everything together to generate referrals from the customers you helped by using Authentic Persuasion.

When you apply the wisdom, skills, strategies, and techniques offered in this book, you will unlock your potential as a sales professional. It's a mental game. If you change your beliefs about how sales are made, and instead focus on maximizing your strengths, you will close more sales, consistently, and in alignment with who you really are. When you embrace what the world truly desires from a salesperson, you will create success and freedom you have never before experienced. That freedom will come in the form of financial success, and in mental peace from using sales efforts as a way to serve your prospects, improve their lives, solve their problems, and help them achieve their goals. When you learn how to be a sales professional, you can go anywhere in the world and use those skills.

I wrote this book because I know the journey you are on, whether you are just thinking about getting into sales or you have been struggling to find success for years. I am the most unlikely person to be writing about how to be a sales superstar. I didn't grow up in a family of salespeople. Before they retired, my mom was in banking and finance and my dad was an engineer. In college, I earned a degree in marine biology. I have taken a very winding path to this point, at times fighting to avoid jobs in sales because I didn't want to be "that guy."

Even with my resistance to being a salesperson, I uncovered that I could truly sell. I have been in sales and sales leadership for seventeen years. I have sold services and products in-person and over the phone. I have helped people get financing, get out of debt, avoid foreclosure, and even grow their businesses. I have coached and trained hundreds of people on how to sell in a way that creates success through doing things the right way, while still being relentlessly effective.

Maybe you think you lack sales success because you don't have a lot of experience. Before I got my first real sales job, I worked in a restaurant washing dishes and prepping food, worked at a pet store, cleaned fish tanks professionally (like the tanks at doctors' and lawyers' offices, Chinese restaurants, and people's homes), waited tables, and worked at Microsoft doing tech support. When I say I never thought I would end up in sales, I mean it!

I am still discovering ways to sell and help others succeed. I will never say I know everything there is to know about sales, persuasion, or human behavior. But I know how to identify when someone is in a sales role but acting like an order taker, and I know how to help them make the shift to sales professional.

I understand if you are unsure if you can, or even want to be, a salesperson. You may be afraid of having to use manipulation and high pressure closing tactics to make money. You are probably hesitant of being a hypocrite, since you wouldn't want to buy from someone like that, and you don't want to do that to others (the Golden Rule!). And I truly understand if you feel like you don't have the stereotypical sales personality traits you think are necessary to be successful.

That is why I wrote this book. I want to be your guide, helping you go from order taker to quota breaker. I know anyone out there who wants to create a successful sales career can take the information in this book and build the life they want. My goal is to be your coach, helping you shift your mindset away from the fears keeping you in order taker mode and moving you to find a level of success and happiness you haven't experienced.

Now, the question that comes up is why someone who says they are amazing at sales writes a book instead of just selling and making lots of money. To be very honest, I love to sell and could make a very good income at it. But I realized years ago that what actually drives me each day is helping salespeople, teams, and companies transform. I love the "light bulb" aha moment when I train or coach someone and they put that information to use and it works to close the sale. Could I sell using Authentic Persuasion and positively impact my customers? Yes, but how many more customers could I help if I taught thousands of salespeople to use Authentic Persuasion? That is my mission and why I wrote this book.

Are you ready to embrace your strengths and core values about how you want to treat people? Are you ready to achieve a level of success in sales you never thought possible? Are you ready to turn yourself into someone who will proudly tell others you are a salesperson because you know the value you truly bring to others?

If so, then now is the time, and this book could be just what you need to top off your sales toolbox with powerful tools to help you in your current sales role or anywhere that life leads you.

SECTION 1
BEING AUTHENTIC

In this first section, my goal is to help you understand what it means to be authentic. And it is hard to come from a place of authenticity unless you are self-aware.

This topic can be the most difficult for people. The first reason is our ego kicks in to protect us. The second reason is it's tough for most people to admit the truth about who they are and aren't. We all have a vision of how great we might be at something; however, stepping outside of that and seeing the truth is the initial, critical step to creating success in anything.

We will start the journey with examining what an order taker is, how to become an authentic salesperson (and why it is so valuable), and where your fears are kicking in to stop you from what you want to create in your sales career. You will notice I mention many times throughout the book the primal parts of the brain that want to keep you safe in your comfort zone. But what you want—your *why*—is on the other side of your comfort zone.

When you are self-aware, authenticity becomes easier. When you step into your sales role as the one who leads the prospect to a better place, then you have succeeded at mastering the first part of the Authentic Persuasion method.

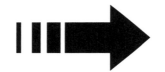

CHAPTER 1

UNCOVERING IF YOU ARE AN ORDER TAKER

"May your choices reflect your hopes, not your fears."

— Nelson Mandela

When Luke talked to prospects, they always sounded so happy. They loved interacting with him. There was just one issue—Luke wasn't closing many sales. Yes, the ones he closed were solid, but each week there weren't enough deals on the board. His client satisfaction surveys might have always been at the top, but he was constantly at the bottom of the performance ranking.

At the time, I had been in Vice President of Sales roles for five years, running inside sales teams initially, moving my way up from sales rep into operational roles and, finally, into sales leadership. When I interviewed Luke for the job, he said all the right things about how he was able to talk to anyone and was driven to close deals and make money. I coached Luke for a few months before I realized why he was not closing more: Luke was an order taker.

In this first chapter of our Authentic Persuasion journey, it is important to start with defining what an order taker is, when it's ideal, and how it leads to sales failure. As a reminder, this discussion is not about what's right or wrong, good or bad. It's about what is true and the best approach relative to the role someone is in.

WHAT IS AN ORDER TAKER?

It might seem self-explanatory, but an order taker is someone who takes orders for a living. The fundamental principle driving the order taker is to be of service, to interact with people based on the goal of helping them fulfil their needs or desires.

An order taker is all about the other person's satisfaction. The order taker is not about ensuring they personally get what they need or want out of the transaction. If it happens—if the order taker does benefit in the end—it will not be due to their strategic effort. They aren't pushing to get what they want or to accomplish their goals.

Transactions between an order taker and another party are not win-win. The order taker will ensure the other person "wins" and feels good about the transaction regardless of whether the order taker experiences any benefit. Order takers, typically, won't push, nag, or try to drive transactions to their own benefit. Win-win is great but win-lose is a more typical, accepted outcome in their mind.

WHEN IS IT APPROPRIATE?

At times, being an order taker is appropriate. In customer service and technical support, an order taker mentality, one where the interaction is all about the other person (customer), is appropriate. Nurturing personalities work really well in those positions. They are the supportive people who just want everyone else to be happy, even if it comes at the cost of their own wellbeing.

If the interaction's goal is to satisfy the other person's needs, wants, or desires, without consideration of your own needs, wants, or desires, then you can assume you are actually an order taker. Of course, there are limits. The checkout person at the grocery store is not your personal servant. They ring you up and send you on your way. You can't just walk up and order them to go get all the items on your list for you while you wait. (Although, funny enough, in most cities you can now have someone who will pick out all your items and either have them ready for you to pick up or deliver them to you.)

Fundamentally, we can all be of service to other people, and we will act as order takers at some point (or maybe even constantly). There is absolutely nothing wrong with serving others, taking orders, or helping people get what they want without benefiting from it. In fact, I would contend that more selfless acts of service are needed in our world.

From a professional standpoint, it is always refreshing to interact with a service person who gives and supports without expectation of benefit—other than a paycheck. It could be the valet who parks your car, or your dry cleaner, or the customer service rep at your bank. In those moments, what you need most is help completing a transaction and getting on your way.

ORDER TAKING GONE BADLY

There are also times when you expect someone to be focused on customer service, but their motivation is more in line with making sales. This experience will be out of alignment from the customer's perspective because it diverges from expectations. Imagine having a salesperson type in a customer service or support role, especially a pushy "closer" personality. They would drive every interaction to meet their own needs, often at the cost of the customer's needs.

We have all experienced "salespeople" in service roles. If you have ever been to an electronics retail store, you probably have dealt with a checkout person relentlessly pushing you to buy the extended warranty. I have dealt with friendly versions where they offer it, and if I say no, they move on, but I have also gone toe to toe with a few who do not want to take no for an answer. I could tell they were driven by either a quota or their own desire to earn bonuses by pushing people to the extended warranty.

This can happen at any service-oriented establishment—your straightforward task turns into something that feels out of place. It's one thing when you walk into a showroom, where you know someone will try to sell you something; it's another when you thought the other person was there just to help you.

WHAT'S WRONG WITH BEING AN ORDER TAKER?

Depending on your situation, nothing may be wrong with being an order taker. The key is what the expectation is for that role. As I mentioned above, if you are in customer service, your goal is to ensure customer satisfaction. Some persuading still occurs in customer service roles. You have to sell the customer on your solution or answer, as well as any upsale opportunities that might enhance their customer experience. Whether an incentive or requirement exists to do so, making cross-sell or upsell suggestions are a part of excellent customer service. It is just important to ensure they do not overshadow the customer-first service goal.

But when you are in a sales role, where your livelihood and job security are based on moving people from prospect to customer, you have to do some selling. Even though most people do not like to be sold to (which I will discuss more in Chapter 6), you have to employ some level of persuasion to achieve success as a sales professional. If you want to win at sales, you cannot just take orders; you must make deals happen.

Unfortunately, that is where a lot of people in sales end up failing. They come into the role with their personality, experiences, and preconceived notions about selling and salespeople. At times, this combination gives them a great start in their sales career by imitating what they have seen. Other times, a sales rep could bring with them the baggage of negative past experiences as a customer, and come in feeling strongly about not wanting to push people into buying. The mindset they develop could grow out of their previous experiences and whether they dealt with someone who used persuasion or manipulation. (I will cover that in Chapter 7.) There is a big difference between the two, but most salespeople who struggle to close deals assume they are the same thing so they avoid either and default to taking orders.

ORDER TAKING EXERCISE

Toward the end of each chapter, I have included a chance for you to rate yourself on the topic. Reading a book is good; underlining, highlighting, and taking notes in the margin will help you absorb more, but taking a few minutes to reflect, do a self-assessment, and maybe write out how you can apply what you learned or where you struggle is even more effective. That's how you will get the most value out of our time together. Most people don't want to write in books (we were taught not to do that when we were given textbooks in grade school), or don't want to take the time, but I strongly encourage you to do so. Don't let this be an interesting book you read, put down, and don't apply to your sales career. Mark it up. Write notes. Draw pictures that help you remember an idea. Do the exercises right in the book. You deserve great results. Do it for yourself and your success.

Are you an order taker or a salesperson? My guess is you are reading this book because your primary responsibility is closing deals, while at the same time, your results might be saying you're taking orders. The big question is: What is your authentic mode?

For this first assessment, where would you honestly put yourself regarding your sales career:

If you didn't rate yourself a 10, what can you use from this chapter to shift to quota breaker?

_____

_____

_____

_____

_____

_____

_____

_____

_____

SUMMARY

I realized Luke mentally operated more like an order taker. He loved talking to people and had no issue striking up conversations. During coaching sessions, he said things like, "I really like helping people." He also said, "I don't like forcing people to buy." That combination is deadly for a sales career. I told Luke the point of the sales professional is to help people achieve their goals, avoid pain, and fundamentally, end up in a better place as a result of dealing with us. I also said we don't want to force anything, but we use certain skills to move people toward purchasing. I told him we are not just hoping for people who show up ready to buy, money in hand, before even talking to us.

Luke faced a mental issue. Dealing with pushy salespeople in the past left him feeling like he didn't want to be "that guy" to his prospects. The result was him going to the other extreme in his current role, where he acted like a customer service rep when he was supposed to be selling. That combination did not work out for Luke. Not just financially, but mentally as well. He constantly felt like a failure. It's unfortunate because his supportive side—driven by his desire to help people—is one of the greatest attributes a salesperson can have.

Our world can always use more people who genuinely want to serve others. They are vital to a more joyful experience as a group. When the situation or role dictates it, being an order taker is just what we all need. But when we expect an order taker and get a sales pitch instead, it is uncomfortable, like something is not right. And when you interact with a salesperson but end up dealing with an order taker, there is a disconnect.

On our Authentic Persuasion journey, the first key step is identifying how you are operating in your sales position. Once you examine your behaviors, you can travel down the path to self-awareness of your authentic self. Do you have the desire to be a successful sales professional? In the next chapter, we will look at the attributes it takes to jump from order taker to quota breaker.

CHAPTER 2

BECOMING AN AUTHENTIC SALESPERSON

"In any given moment we have two options: to step forward into growth or step back into safety."

— Abraham Maslow

Like most kids, Kimberly went through many phases of what she wanted to be when she grew up. From doctor to archaeologist, scientist to therapist, each of her career fantasies centered on making discoveries, solving problems, or helping people in some way. Yet when I met her, she was in her thirties, married, had a young son, and was working in a sales position.

Some people seem to be natural-born salespeople, with the ability to even sell sand in the desert, as the saying goes. It feels like those people won the lottery for using charisma and wit to effortlessly talk anyone into anything. They seem to be great storytellers who have an anecdote for everything.

I could definitely relate to Kimberly in both her early career dreams and where she had ended up when I met her. Some people might assume you have to be a natural born salesperson to be successful—either you were given the gift of selling or you weren't. My experience of Kimberly was someone who had become amazing at sales, could easily converse with any prospect, was very open to learning, and never gave up. In this chapter, I am going to explore what I have learned about how a seemingly unnatural salesperson can create a great career in sales by leveraging certain key attributes.

Now that we are on the same page about what an order taker is and how being one can show up as a detriment to a successful sales career, let's talk about the other elephant in the room: Can anyone become a sales superstar? I have worked with, coached, trained, and led hundreds and hundreds of salespeople, and I truly believe there is no simple formula or model. There are, however, some common attributes in the successful salespeople I have seen.

NATURE AND NURTURE

Is it just me, or does it seem like every sales trainer guru out there is telling people they don't have to be born a salesperson, yet the guru is all about using charisma and charm, and telling stories about how they have been in sales their whole life? The real question comes down to: How much of a determinant for sale success is based on the personality traits someone is born with and how much is a factor of what happens during their life? I feel both are important, but neither are limiting: you can become a great salesperson whether you are born with the skills or you develop them along the way.

Personally, neither nature nor nurture was in my favor. I was not gifted with ultra-charismatic communication or selling skills. I didn't grow up in a "House of Sales" with parents or siblings who sold things for a living. Yet here I am having developed certain selling skills, abilities, and instincts from seemingly nothing. That personal experience is the fundamental basis for why I wrote this book. And why I believe anyone interested in becoming a professional salesperson can do so.

Besides being in sales and sales management roles myself, I have seen a lot of different people enter sales roles with the goal of finding a new career and making money. I have also seen an equally large number of people leave sales roles because they couldn't create success. While, without doubt, some personality characteristics lend themselves perfectly to sales, this book is not written for perfect salespeople. Therefore, I want to share the less obvious, but potentially more effective traits and behaviors. I have found that you need five traits to be a successful salesperson. Those traits are:

1. Be open and willing.
2. Be curious.
3. Be persistent.
4. Be creative
5. Be authentic

Let's take a few minutes to look at each of these traits in detail.

BE OPEN AND WILLING

Being an effective salesperson requires a useful, productive level of ego—the kind where confidence comes through in everything you say and do. A less productive ego is the kind that gets in the way of the person's ability or desire to take constructive feedback, get help in small or big ways, or be open to new things. Every successful salesperson I have met is open to improvement. They do not think they know everything. They have a healthy balance of ego.

I have never met someone who thought they were "God's gift to sales" who was actually good at being a sales professional. Maybe they were good at manipulating small numbers of people into buying, but manipulation is not a sustainable, long-term selling strategy. Maybe they appeared to be sales superstars, but without being open to new information or feedback, their techniques would not translate into consistent results in other verticals. I have seen a lot of one-trick-pony sales professionals who would struggle to succeed at selling anything beyond what they currently know.

Openness means not prejudging a situation, person, or piece of information based on previous experience or external influences. In sales, being open to learning from others' successes and acknowledging feedback with the goal of improving are fundamental for short- and long-term success.

Willingness can come to you naturally or be a learned skill. The goal is to approach life from a more open/willing place with a healthy ego. A salesperson's willing attitude will lead them to do more—to take on new challenges—and it goes together with openness. When you are open to feedback or learning a new skill and then willing to use that information to achieve more or different results, you will win at the game of sales. Willingness is essentially a motivated openness, but you can't stop there. I laugh every time I read the Jim Rohn quote: "Motivation alone is not enough. If you have an idiot and you motivate him, now you have a motivated idiot." It is funny but very accurate. Success comes from combining motivation with knowledge, experience, and learning.

BE CURIOUS

Curiosity is an important personality trait that goes hand in hand with willingness. If you are naturally inquisitive, it will help you deal with prospects (see Chapter 10: Asking Questions). Your curiosity might come from a fascination with how things work. Perhaps you like to solve problems, so when you see something that could be a "puzzle," you want to dive in to solve it. Curiosity will serve as your guide on the path to wisdom.

When selling a product or service, the best thing you can do is be curious about your prospect's situation, and whatever issue, pain point, challenge, or goal they have that you could potentially solve. I have more of a problem-solving mindset, where my curiosity and questions come from a place of wanting to know details and truths, and then I try to see how I can help make things better. How can I put the pieces of the prospect's "puzzle" together to help them? Being curious and seeking knowledge are not just about sales success, but life success.

In your selling career, spend time learning about your business, product/service, and industry. Even after you become a "pro," always stay open to learning new things. Constantly read sales books and watch sales videos. No matter how long I have been in sales, I am constantly learning new techniques and skills to add to my selling toolbox, especially from sales training completely outside my current industry. There are always good strategies and scripts you can borrow, tweak, and apply for your focus. (Caution: An abundance of bad sales advice also exists, so make sure you analyze and filter what you take in!)

My goal isn't to fill this book with the perfect questions and responses to get you a sale every time. Tons of resources are out there for that. If you are unsure where to start, I recommend getting your hands on anything by Zig Ziglar or Jim Rohn, and then exploring other sales experts with a wide range of topics and techniques (Jeffrey Gitomer, Victor Antonio, etc.). Just never stop learning. If you struggle with wanting to learn more, do your best to grow your curiosity muscles.

BE PERSISTENT

It might seem obvious, but persistence is key to success. Of course, as a winning salesperson, you need to be tenacious and persistent. No good salesperson gives up easily or often; everyone knows that. But there are a few different areas where persistence and tenacity are most important.

First, never give up on your selling career. There will be tough days full of rejection, days you just don't want to keep at it. The people who get up and go in every day anyway will win long term. Steven Pressfield talks about being a "professional" in your career, similar to how a professional athlete shows up each and every day—no matter what. If you can still go when you are tired, unhappy, or just generally don't feel like it, while giving it your best effort when you feel your worst, you will outperform even the "natural" salespeople who try to get by on talent alone.

Slumps happen all the time in sales, as they do in sports. For any sales professional, slumps will be a recurring thing during their career, not a one-time event. Do you have the deeper drive and character to keep taking and making calls, knocking on doors, and talking to people even if it's been a day, a week, or a month since your last sale? Can you enter into an interaction with a new prospect with faith and confidence in yourself and in your product/service? Tenacity, the persistence to keep trying, is key to your sales career, particularly when you aren't winning.

Lastly, tenacity is critical when you have a prospect you know you can help. If you have a never-give-up attitude when it comes to getting to the heart of their issues (see Chapter 10: Asking Questions), and you care about them (see Chapter 3 on caring), and you keep providing solutions until they get what they want or need, then you will win long term. If your prospects throw obstacles at you (they need to talk to their spouse, they don't have their bank information with them, they don't have access to the internet, and so on), will you switch to problem solver, obstacle overcomer mode until the sale is done?

BE CREATIVE

When I used to hear the word creativity, I only thought of painters, sculptors, actors, and musicians. Then I realized everyone has a creative side, even if rarely used, and even if not in a classical *art* sense. Successful salespeople use creativity in their process to facilitate closing the sale. Being creative is about trusting yourself and what you know, then letting go of control so the creative part can flow through.

Creativity is an important tool in two main sales areas. The first is in the conversation and dialogue. When used at a higher level, creativity allows a salesperson to ask questions, listen to their replies, take in objections or issues from the prospect, and respond in the optimal way. Sales reps who struggle with creativity will have difficulty thinking on their feet and providing a useful, valuable reply instead of just a loop of the same lines or responses.

Creativity is also vital in overcoming barriers. Most sales interactions will have some kind of issue, ranging from small speed bumps to brick walls. If they were all easy, it wouldn't require salespeople. These barriers could be money, document access, or needing approval from another party. Being creative is about finding solutions to that sales impediment so the transaction can be completed. There is always a solution, but the question is: Will you find it?

BE AUTHENTIC

The final trait in the list is to be authentic. To me, being authentic is the most important one, but it's also the hardest for most people to use. I won't go into detail here because we will spend the rest of the first section building on this authentic side, its value, and the challenges that prevent it. But I will say there is so much power in being authentic in your sales role. The more authentic, more real, more human you are with your prospects, the more the persuasion piece will feel easy.

BECOMING A SALESPERSON

When you employ the five above traits you have an amazing head start that could lead to a great sales career. If you are missing some, do not worry because, in my opinion, they are all learnable. Looking at myself as an example, I feel like I was naturally curious, but not when it came to people. Growing up as a shy, only child left me feeling a little weird and socially awkward. It wasn't until after high school that I started to really deal with people in a work environment. My first real sales role didn't come until I was twenty-seven. And I didn't learn the art of selling until I was in my mid-thirties.

Every new sales role has required me to push myself in uncomfortable ways, forcing me either to adapt and learn or fail. One of the most difficult traits to develop was the willingness to accept feedback, to be wrong, to change. Most people do not like being told they are doing something incorrectly. I know I don't enjoy it, or at least I didn't while I was growing up. But over the years, I realized how important it is to accept constructive feedback focused on helping me improve.

I was also not born with an overly tenacious personality. Honestly, my default mode is to give up when things get hard. When a puzzle, video game, or brain teaser starts to feel impossible, I usually stop and move on to something else—something easier, where I can feel like I'm winning. But in sales, you cannot do that—well, not for very long—and still keep your job. You can't just wait for prospects who come to you with money in their outstretched hands ready to pay top dollar for whatever you are selling with no questions asked. Yes, those buyers, known as "laydowns," do exist, and you will encounter a certain number of them over time, but you cannot build a reliable and successful sales career on the backs of laydowns.

Dealing with prospects' needs is complex and difficult, and I learned if I gave up when it got tough, or when they said no, I was not living up to my potential; I was not doing my job. More importantly, I would be letting that person down by not serving them completely. I have learned not to give up during a transaction. For years, I had to remind myself to be tenacious and persistent until it became a habit and part of my personality. Now I see my role in sales as a duty to others.

BECOMING AN AUTHENTIC SALESPERSON EXERCISE

I know we are just starting this journey together, but let's get real right out of the gate. Hopefully, that's what you are here for—some valuable self-discovery and to maximize who you are. So, let's go as deep as we can right away. Below I have listed the traits described in this chapter with space next to each for you to write how you would rate yourself in each category, how well you do at it, and what you could do to improve. There is also a section for you to fill in any other traits or behaviors that come to mind that may be hidden strengths you have. My goal is to support you in looking at all of the most effective ways to be the best salesperson possible, maximizing all your traits, even the ones that aren't thought of as strengths in sales.

	Nope, not at all										Hell, yes!
	0	1	2	3	4	5	6	7	8	9	10
Open											
Curious											
Persistent											
Curious											
Authentic											

Other traits/notes: _____

_____

_____

_____

SUMMARY

Turns out, Kimberly was doing well in sales. The funny part is that it really surprised her. She never guessed life would take her on this path and she would be persuading people to buy things every day. Yet, here she was, helping her prospects, solving problems, and being tenacious. She attributed her success to being open and curious. She didn't know where her life would go next, but she was enjoying her sales success.

I wrote this book based on my journey and those of people like Kimberly I have had the pleasure of meeting. These experiences center on the fact that many people have never thought of themselves as salespeople, yet have not only entered a sales field, but embraced it and learned how to make themselves sales superstars. I know this will sound cliché, like something on a late-night infomercial, but I truly feel if I can do it, so can anyone else who wants to. It's not about being a "certain" person; it's about maximizing who you are (see Chapter 5: Acknowledging Your Strengths)—especially when it is your true authentic self.

These traits—openness, curiosity, tenaciousness, creativity, and being true to yourself—in combination are a winning formula for your selling career and life in general. They, along with your unique personality and experiences, are a great foundation for dealing with prospective buyers. Even if you do not possess these traits, you can always develop them over time. As Anais Nin said, "Life is a process of becoming, a combination of states we have to go through. Where people fail is that they wish to elect a state and remain in it. This is a kind of death."

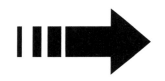

CHAPTER 3

ADMITTING YOUR FEARS

"The biggest rewards in life are found outside of your comfort zone. Live with it. Fear and risk are prerequisites if you want to enjoy a life of success and adventure."

— Jack Canfield

I could feel the hesitation coming from Jennifer. It was almost like there was a stressed aura cloud around her. If you paid close enough attention, you could see her muscles tighten as she pressed the buttons to make a call. The most interesting part was, in person, she seemed confident, outgoing, and personable. But when it came to making sales calls, she was pretty much paralyzed with fear.

Whether it was calling a prospect back to finalize the paperwork or reaching out to someone who filled out a lead form on the website, the hesitation was the same. That crippling fear would end Jennifer's sales career if she didn't do something about it.

In the last chapter, we discussed how to become an authentic salesperson. In that process, certain traits will come to you naturally, and a handful you can develop over time. We all have our strengths—the ones we were born with or have developed over time.

If we each have our strengths and have survived every day of our lives so far, what do we really have to be afraid of? Why was Jennifer, like so many other salespeople, hesitant to pick up the phone to make calls? Where does this fear come from?

In this chapter, we will look into human behavior, psychology, and mindset to help us identify where this fear started. Authenticity is on the other side of the fears holding you back.

OUR PRIMITIVE BRAIN

My guess and hope is that, if you are reading this book, your life is fairly comfortable. You probably have a roof over your head, some sort of transportation, easy and consistent access to safe food and clean water, and clothes on your back. Tens of thousands of years ago, life was a bit different for us *homo sapiens*. The lucky ones had a nice, cozy shelter to live in that provided some level of protection from the elements. For those lucky few, survival was just left hinging on little things like eating the wrong things and dying of food poisoning, or cuts, scrapes, and broken bones that could kill us via infection. Oh, and there were all those wild creatures that wanted to eat us.

Because our species survived in many harsh environments and situations for millennia, we developed an area of our brain focused only on survival. That primitive part still exists in each of us. We are hardwired to survive. Survival comes from the fine balance between playing it safe, flying under the radar, and taking action at the right time, yielding the biggest benefit with the least risk.

Way back in the day, an individual's longevity was a matter of picking the right berry, shelter, and prey, psychology, and mindset while knowing which ones could kill you. The fascinating part is that same portion of our primitive brain still thinks one careless move means certain death.

COMFORT ZONE

Obviously, we humans persevered by learning what was safe and what was not. Over thousands of years, our brains created something we usually refer to as our "comfort zone." Today, our comfort zone is made up of the people, places, and things we feel are safe.

For many, safe equals staying in their hometown, eating foods they grew up with, traveling to familiar places, going to the same restaurants, and talking to people they already know. The reliable and known reduce stress or risk in our mind. Traveling to new and different places, talking to strangers, and doing new activities all trigger discomfort in the brain and signal a potentially unsafe situation.

The most interesting part is how our brains react to situations that seem unsafe and are outside of our comfort zone. We are wired to either fight, flee, or freeze. Depending on our inherent risk tolerance, our brain will trigger the same fight, flight, or freeze reaction as if we were being run down by a top-of-the-food-chain predator ten thousand years ago, even if we are just trying to discuss our sales pipeline in a meeting with our manager. But there are no saber-tooth tigers trying to kill most people anymore. In fact, there is very little to actually be "afraid" of when living in a First World country. Yet our brain wants to keep us in our comfort zone, safe from prehistoric harm, so we can survive long enough to procreate.

When you really look at it logically, fears make sense. In the wild, it would be better for our mind to see danger around every corner and play tricks on us, even if it's wrong. At least then we would still be alive versus thinking everything is great and safe and being wrong, even once. Not seeing that tiger could lead to a worse outcome for us than imagining every moving shadow we see could be a danger.

We have all met or read about someone who seems to be comfortable in any situation. Such people are huge risk-takers; they will do or try anything, talk to anyone, and seem to have no limits. These individuals have found a way to push (or completely ignore) the boundaries of normal comfort zones. As the quote says, "Feel the fear and do it anyway." The daredevils who will go skydiving, bungee jumping, or swimming with sharks all still feel fear. They just don't let it stop them.

Think about karaoke singing. Many people would never think about getting on a stage to sing karaoke in front of people, at least not sober. That falls under the same category as people's fear of public speaking. However, mix in some "liquid courage" (alcohol) and lots of people feel a wave of bravery wash over them. Their comfort zone's boundaries temporarily change, fear levels go down, tolerances for risk go up—inhibitions fall away. Of course, there are people who do karaoke sober and others who enjoy public speaking. Many of these people who are more comfortable singing or speaking in public still feel the fear, but they're pretty sure they won't die from rocking out to "Bohemian Rhapsody," and they do it despite the fear.

WHAT ARE YOU AFRAID OF?

So why am I talking about our cave-dwelling ancestors, comfort zones, and fears in a book about sales? Because those primal survival instincts can paralyze a salesperson. Most people don't even realize what is causing them to hesitate in picking up the phone, sending an email to a prospect, or moving a conversation toward the sale. In observing salespeople, I've seen that the outward symptoms are the actions of an order taker waiting for the safety of a prospect with money in hand asking to buy. That is safe to the salesperson—very little chance of rejection, embarrassment, or hurt feelings. Asking for the sale, making outbound calls, or anything else that could lead to being told no or getting yelled at will subconsciously feel unsafe. Order takers like being safely in their comfort zones where nothing will harm them.

What are you really afraid of? What is the worst that could happen? The prospect tells you no and hangs up on you? They don't buy from you? They complain to your manager? They write a bad review about you online?

Most people put public speaking at the top of their list of fears, usually tied with or above death. Why is it so scary? The answer is actually really simple and logical. As we discussed, our primitive brains were trained over millennia to stay safe by living within our comfort zones (comfort = safe, change = death). But another big motivator is we have always been a social, tribal species. There is safety in groups. If we got kicked out of the tribe, it meant facing the elements and animals on our own, which was most likely fatal. Our ancestors needed to go along to get along because the alternative to community was death.

Of course, everyone has a different comfort zone, but most people's brains tell them to fear public speaking, cold calling, talking to random strangers—any situations that could lead to rejection.

And if our "tribe" rejects us, we could end up alone. Of course, talking to a random person in line at the grocery store won't get you banished into the mountains, but our brain doesn't think that way. While we logically know if we give a speech—even if we are mocked and ridiculed, and feel embarrassed and maybe ashamed—we won't be voted out of our neighborhood or the human race, we still hesitate to go beyond our comfort zone.

These fears, given to us by that survival instinct part of the brain, loosely based on reality or actual experiences, are the barrier keeping you from achieving what you want in life. Instead of being your authentic self—mistakes, failures, triumphs, and passions—if you are like most people, you let fear limit you.

CONFIDENCE

Typically, fear is the result of a lack of confidence. *Dictionary. com* defines confidence as "a feeling of self-assurance arising from one's appreciation of one's own abilities or qualities." When you can appreciate your strengths and the value you bring to a certain situation, task, or role, then the belief in yourself will be higher. Even if you do not feel that way in your sales role, my guess is you feel confident in at least one other area in life. It could be cooking, or a particular sport, or trivia knowledge, or in relationships, or world traveling, or mountain biking. The key is to recognize where you feel powerful in your abilities and find a way to do the same in your sales career.

Your goal is to have confidence in yourself as a sales professional. Confidence will help you push past the fears holding you captive in your comfort zone. It is the key to realizing there is truly nothing to be afraid of in most situations. (You may still have a little fear about bungee-jumping and sky-diving, but confidence in the process, equipment, and skills will help a bunch.) Confident people will jump up on that stage, or make that call, or walk up to that person and start a conversation, for they truly understand and believe no harm will come to them. As the saying goes: Feel the fear and do it anyway. Make your confidence greater than your fears.

SCARY EXERCISE

How much does fear affect your sales activities?

If you didn't rate yourself a 10, what can you use from this chapter to keep fear from limiting your success?

_____

_____

_____

_____

_____

_____

_____

_____

Where do your self-limiting fears get in the way of your sales
success? Where is your mind trying to keep you safe, to the detriment of your sales career?

_____

_____

_____

_____

_____

_____

SUMMARY

It turns out what paralyzed Jennifer was fear of rejection. When we talked about what it would really mean if someone told her no, she recalled being young and asking kids in her neighborhood to play and them saying no. Those hurt feelings were still buried deep in her subconscious. As she focused on the abilities she had, it built a level of confidence that helped her see the ridiculousness of her fears and how easy it would be to do what she was holding herself back from.

Of course, there are still things to be afraid of in our society (like people driving while looking at their phones). But for most people, there is no saber-toothed tiger waiting to ambush them on their way to work. And while our minds want us to believe it is better to shy away from seemingly treacherous situations, we would have to do some pretty bad things to officially be banished from the population. Yet, we all have fears that drive us to stay within our comfort zones. Our primitive brains feel safest there, even if it no longer applies.

For salespeople, our subconsciously hardwired fears that are intended to keep us safe could potentially be detrimental to our success. Sales superstars feel their fears but press forward anyway. They have learned that those fears are unreasonable and do not support their winning goals. Hiding who they really are out of fear won't get them where they want to go. In my experience, superstars feed off the challenge of proving these fears wrong.

Confidence is the secret weapon to move past fears in our sales career. Your goal is to acknowledge your fears, embrace your abilities, and move forward in a confident way. If you are struggling with that, look to other areas in your life where you feel empowered and bring that with you into selling. Another good way to build confidence is by embodying the five traits from the previous chapter.

In the next chapter, we will talk about the best way to overpower those fears, and how to shift into action by being in touch with why we are in sales.

CHAPTER 4

FOCUSING ON WHY YOU ARE SELLING

"There is one quality which one must possess to win, and that is definiteness of purpose, the knowledge of what one wants, and a burning desire to possess it."

— Napoleon Hill

Now that Jennifer was able to define her fears and put them into a big picture perspective, she realized there was actually little to fear. While that revelation seemed to help, knowing the reason for her fears and having a name for them was only the first, small step. While she improved, you could see she still held herself back from making calls and moving prospects forward to the sale.

The issue was that Jennifer didn't know what to focus on instead of her fears to push past them.

In the last chapter, we discussed the primal fears that are quite misplaced in our current, comfortable society. I am not saying no one should fear anything, but most fears are a legacy of our primitive survival mechanism to stay alive in a world where many things were trying to kill us or a defense mechanism that remembers painful experiences from our past and wants to keep us sheltered from anything else that might hurt our feelings. A big difference exists between the actual survival instinct and our hesitation to make a phone call that could lead to being rejected.

(I remember the feeling of pure dread before calling someone to ask them out on a date and the rejection scenarios that ran through my mind as the phone rang.) You might remember the popular '90s phrase "No Fear." Well, I suggest the first step is actually to Know Fear. Borrowing from most addiction treatment groups: The first step is admitting you have a problem. Then you can do something about it.

How can you take action in the face of fear? How do you fight against generations of hardwiring keeping you in your comfort zone? The answer is simple, and of course, not always easy: Focus on your *why*. In this chapter, we explore what *why* is, and how to use *why* as a tool for success in sales and in leading a more joyful life. Your success in sales lies on the other side of your comfort zone. I will help you find that roadmap to get there.

WHY A *WHY* MATTERS

Why does *why* even matter in the first place? And what the heck is a *why*? You might also be wondering if this is the point in the book where I try to go all self-help guru on you and get spiritual about a higher purpose and the meaning of life. Self-help guru— no. Meaning of life—maybe. Higher purpose—sort of.

Let's start with what having a *why* means. Your *why* drives the decisions you make. By default, most people don't have a *why* and end up going through life more like a leaf in the wind than like a driver following GPS directions toward a specific destination. I am not going to go into great detail about understanding your *why* in terms of your life's purpose and focus and how to live based on your *why*—there are so many great books out there that already cover the subject. (One place to start is Simon Sinek's *Start With Why*.)

What I do want to focus on is your *why* when it comes to whatever you are selling. Your *why* helps align your focus with your actions and, hopefully, leads to the results you want. When you are clear on your *why*, certain decisions become easier, like which actions to take as a salesperson and what to avoid that will not get you where you want to be.

Having a *why* can also be the difference between pushing through obstacles and quitting on a task or goal. Fundamentally, when you want something different, it will cause you to change your actions and mindset, moving you out of your comfort zone. It's called the comfort zone because it's comfortable and safe, which is why we resist changing the way we do. To offset that feeling of fear or resistance, you want to have a *why* that will drive you through the wall of comfort your mind has built around you.

Having a *why* will also help you see the bigger picture, the bigger game you are playing. When you step back and identify what matters most, you will begin to step up as your authentic self more, and push aside the fears holding you back, or worse, tricking you into acting like someone you are not. We have all met people who were driven by a *why* or goal, and they usually come across as very authentic. Being in touch with your *why* will create a powerful authenticity inside that will fuel your sales conversations, whether your prospects even know what your *why* is.

YOUR *WHY*

For many years, I have had all my new sales reps create a vision board. I provide them with a fourteen-inch square piece of corkboard as the blank canvas. Their instructions are simple: find images or quotes on the internet, in magazines, or from their own pictures and attach as many as they want to create an emotional mosaic on the corkboard. The goal is to create a visual representation of the things that motivate them.

The vision board exercise is designed to answer the question: "What will drive you to make the fifty-first phone call of the day?" After you have made fifty phone calls for the day, and no one has answered and you have left fifty voicemail or heard dozens of nos, you have two choices: quit calling and consider the day a lost cause, or keep calling until you run out of phone numbers or hours at the office.

What I know to be true is that the classic sales management method is: the carrot and the stick. Positive reinforcement, praise, money, trips, President's Club, or threats, performance meetings, warnings, and terminations. Short term, those can work to motivate, but long term, they are never sustainable. The more effective way to succeed in sales is to be intrinsically motivated by something inside of you that you want. When you know what that is, and why, your sales career will feel much easier.

What is your *why*? It might sound cliché, but what gets you out of bed each day? What do you want to accomplish, buy, have, and do, or where do you want to go and what do you want to be that would motivate you to push through uncomfortable times, obstacles, rejection, and fears? As Les Brown explains, "Wanting something is not enough. You must hunger for it. Your motivation must be absolutely compelling in order to overcome the obstacles that will invariably come your way."

NOT ALWAYS ABOUT MONEY

Many people feel their *why* needs to be focused on money or purchasing a certain item. That's what our consumer media and society is constantly telling us—there is something out there we must buy to be happy and feel fulfilled. I am not saying that is wrong—there are times when we will have important goals that require a certain accumulation of money to be achieved. Especially in sales, money is the scoreboard of your success in creative value and solving problems. Money is necessary and a good thing to have, yet not everyone's main motivator.

Let me share my *why*. When I was in high school, my parents pushed me to go to college. They wanted me to be the first one in our family to get a degree. They knew it would allow me many more choices than they'd had in their careers. I was a late-bloomer and not totally emotionally ready for college, so I went to the local community college for a few years, and then I went to University of California at Santa Cruz, where I earned a degree in marine biology. I have never used my degree and have made my way through life sampling many different industries and jobs. Not until I was thirty-eight did I realize what I wanted to be when I grew up.

I beat myself up for most of my adult life thinking I didn't do it *right*: go to college, get a degree, use that degree, work in that field, advance, and make a career out of it. Then I realized everything I had gone through, including my work experience, made me into the person I am, allowing me to help a wide range of people with a diverse set of problems. I wouldn't change my life path, but I wish someone along the way had helped me recognize how valuable my special intersection of skills, talents, abilities, and experiences were. I am now totally driven by helping other people identify who they are, what drives them, what makes them special, how to maximize their strengths and passions, and how to get through life's struggles, and facilitating that aha moment.

Throughout our life, the work we do and what drives us to get up each day will come from different *why* motivations. It could come from a place we may or may not be able to verbalize. There is nothing wrong with having nice cars, big houses, and tropical locations on your vision board (I have all that on mine)—these are good rewards for a job well done. However, you may find when you continue down a path of self-discovery and self-awareness that your *why* shifts over time, maybe even to a unique sense of duty and responsibility to yourself and others.

NO JUDGMENT

Now, if you don't know what your bigger purpose is, and you are just focused on making money to fund the goals you have, great—there is nothing wrong with that at all. We all have different seasons, all with their own unique priorities. Our goals can go from working toward buying a house to, later on, selling everything to travel for a year, living out of a backpack, without having to work.

Through years of managing sales teams, I have learned that one big key to having a *why* and making a vision board is to banish self-judgment about your goals and focus. One of my top performers for years was a single mother with two kids. She didn't have a choice—she had to be successful. She had no other option than to make as much money as she could each day. Since the number of hours she could work each day was limited due to childcare options, availability, and cost, she also had no choice but to make the most out of the time she was in the office. Her *why* was super-obvious to everyone in the office, and her activity level each week reflected that.

I tell this story because I had many people who passed judgment on items on their vision board, labeling many goals as "not important." Because they weren't single parents, didn't have kids, or a family, or they already owned a house, they felt like their *why* wasn't good enough. But this is the key for your *why*—it's *your why*, not anyone else's. It's critical that you avoid judgment, be true to what matters to you, and not compare it to anyone else. Theodore Roosevelt is credited with saying "Comparison is the thief of joy." That is so true, especially when we talk about goals, hopes, dreams, and purpose. If you are negatively judging your *why*, ask yourself if you are being authentic.

Please know that your goal of making and saving enough money to move out of your parents' house, your goal of buying a new car, or your goal of going on a vacation is just as important as someone else's goal to support a family, own a home, or save money to go to college. Remember, all our paths are unique, and fundamentally, everyone is in a different season of their life. Pictures of the next car you want to buy, or the beach you want to travel to and sit on for a week, or the money you want saved in the bank as your financial cushion, or the big TV you want in your living room are the perfect *why* if that's what is true for you at this moment.

MISCELLANEOUS *WHY* RECOMMENDATIONS

Before we move on, I want to discuss a few final rules I am putting under "miscellaneous." The first is that your *why*, and even what you feel is your life's purpose, will shift over time. As I mentioned, there are points in your life when the most important thing might be that large TV, buying a house, a vacation, or getting rid of everything and traveling for a year. I read and listen to a lot of self-help gurus who push people to determine their life's purpose—their *big why*—and then focus on that. But I think that is bad advice for the population at large.

Like I said, I didn't really figure out what I wanted to be when I grew up until I was thirty-eight, and ever since then, it has continued to shift and evolve. I know my purpose will probably change as I get older, experience more, learn more, and become an even better version of myself. Always focus on what feels right for you and where you are at this moment. Don't put too much pressure on knowing what you should do with the rest of your life. And be open to going wherever life takes you and your goals.

The second *why* recommendation is relative to how much power it will take to achieve your *why*. The bigger the goal, the bigger the *why* you want behind it pushing you through. A giant goal requires you to do things differently; it forces you to do uncomfortable things. Your brain will play tricks on you and do its best to convince you to stop doing risky, uncomfortable, "dangerous" things. To persevere, you need a *big why* to match your big goal. If your *why* starts with, "It would be nice to...," then it's most likely not strong enough to drive you through the walls your mind will build to keep you "safe." Instead, do your best to find a *why* that is important to you; your dialogue around this big why (internal or external) starts with, "I will be/do/have...." The more the images on your vision board energize you at a deeper level when you look at them, the more likely you are to make that fifty-first phone call, or knock on that hundredth door, or go to that networking event and actually talk to strangers. The stronger you feel about your *why*, the more likely you are to achieve it.

Finally, no matter what your *why* is, long-term success in your profession will come when you are driven by your goals, but not at the expense of your customers' best interests. When your motivation and goals come before the other person's needs or desires, then you are operating on shaky ground. The classic example most people think of is the stereotypical *used car* salesperson. (Note: This is a common mental image, but it's not fair to assume all used car salespeople have bad intentions.) Their goal is to sell a car to anyone who walks onto the lot. The vision in our collective imagination is a high pressure, slick pitch aimed at selling whichever car the manager said needs to go—probably a piece of junk that will, in fact, break down shortly after you drive it off the lot. That salesperson's goals far exceed any concerns for the buyer's happiness and satisfaction. This kind of tactic and one-sided experience has been around longer than cars have, as most people assume will occur.

The best way to avoid being *that person* is to come from a place of abundance. There are more than enough people to sell your product or service to. Manipulating someone to buy may work in the short-term, but it isn't a good long-term strategy (which we will cover in Section 2). Some interesting subconscious things also happen when you approach selling from a place of scarcity, a self-centered place. The result? You come across as desperate. When your motivation is purely your own needs, the other person will sense it through your words and actions. Most of us have had an experience where we encountered a salesperson and could *feel* the desperation oozing off them. We might buy from them, anyway, because we want the item badly enough, but we definitely do not buy because of a selfish sales pitch.

Once, when I was managing a sales team, my boss decided to motivate the team to close more deals that day, so he walked out on the floor and taped five $100 bills to the wall, telling us, for each deal we closed, we could grab $100 off the wall. Normally, we handed out ten or twenty bucks extra per deal as a special spiff, so this got the team buzzing with excitement. With that big carrot dangling from the wall, you might assume we broke all our sales records that day.

Actually, the opposite happened—from that moment until the end of the day, we closed zero deals. When I listened to the team's conversations with customers, what had happened became obvious—the team's focus had gone from trying to help people by saying and doing the right things to emitting high-pressure, forceful desperation that pushed away each person they spoke with. That cash on the wall killed all the deals for the rest of the day.

I share this cautionary tale because it is important to always have your *why* in place, your vision board on the wall or in your mind, and feel the energy of what gets you up in the morning as deeply as possible *and* operate within each conversation from a place of service to the other person (persuasion). If your new car or tropical vacation has to come as a result of manipulating others to get what you want, it will be hard to sustain long term.

YOUR *WHY* EXERCISE

How well do you know your why and is it a powerful driver for your success?

If you didn't rate yourself a 10, what can you use from this chapter to identify your most powerful motivator?

_____

_____

_____

_____

_____

_____

_____

_____

_____

_____

SUMMARY OF *WHY*

Jennifer spent some time thinking about her life and what really made her happy. She realized that what drove her to strive for success was a need to create financial security. She didn't like the thought of failing and having to live in her parents' basement for the rest of her life (which, of course, wouldn't happen, but that was what it felt like), so she wanted a level of financial success that would maintain her independence. This didn't mean buying a big house, or a fancy car, but the peace of mind of knowing that, if anything did go wrong with her job, her health, or the world, she would be okay for a while. That was her *why* in this particular season of her life and what got her out of bed energized and ready to focus on closing sales.

One understated, yet key component to your selling success will be your connection with the *why* that drives you. Your goal is to identify the *why* that is strong enough to have you jumping out of bed each morning with excitement as opposed to staying stuck from fear. That may be far from your current motivation level. Unfortunately, most people don't make it their goal to have a job they actually look forward to. Of course, I would love for each person reading this to be excited by their life and career, but don't judge yourself too harshly if you have to take baby steps toward that vision.

For whatever you are selling (your ideas to your boss, room cleaning to your kids, or furniture to a young couple), make sure you have a *why* that drives you. The bigger the *why*, the better. This will create motivation from within that will be much more powerful than any external force. It will also be the key to move past those fears that are keeping you from what you want. And make sure you do not judge or compare your *why* to other people's because everyone is in a different season of life. There is no right or wrong *why*—there is only what is true for you and what fires you up to perform at an amazingly higher level. As your life moves forward, don't be surprised when your *why* changes and your goals shift. And try not to pick a *why* just to please someone else.

No matter what, do not let your *why* overshadow the wellbeing and goals of the person you are potentially selling to. Short term, you can get results in transactions where others must lose for you to win, but long term, salespeople who operate like that will not do well. As Gary Vaynerchuk said, "Doing the right thing is always the right thing to do."

Now that you know why you want to be successful, in the next chapter, we will start the process of helping you achieve that success. Success doesn't come from changing who you are to be like someone else. It's about becoming self-aware, then going all in on your strengths. This will be the foundation your sales career and success are built upon. I hope you are ready to start winning by being who you were meant to be.

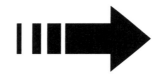

CHAPTER 5

ACKNOWLEDGING YOUR STRENGTHS

"Success is not measured by what you do compared to what others do; it is measured by what you do with the ability God gave you."

— Zig Ziglar

Ben sat across from me in my office looking frustrated and disappointed. He wasn't hitting his numbers, and he knew it. He couldn't avoid the facts since he was the one who sat in the sales room, day in and day out, and felt like everyone else around him was closing deals. While I knew his numbers weren't that bad compared to the team's stats, I understood why he thought he was performing poorly. Sitting next to Carl definitely didn't help.

Carl was on track to have an amazing sales year. Ben knew it because every time he turned around, Carl was ringing the sales bell. Ben sat in front of me looking for help. He wondered if sales might not be the right career for him. Ben figured he didn't have the gift of talking people into buying.

In the last few chapters, we went from looking at deeply imbedded, hardwired fears we all have to identifying the most powerful tool to overcome those fears. When you are connected to your *why* (remember that your *why* could be a big picture, lifetime purpose, or whatever drives you at this single moment), then hopefully, your fears will pale in comparison to your bigger reason to take action.

Now, I want to help you take your *why* and see how it's possible to win by being authentic to who you are, not who anyone else is. One of the biggest problems plaguing people since the beginning of time is comparing themselves to what others have or do. This is not just a new issue with the internet, social media, and an ultra-connected world. We have been either pushing ourselves or feeling bad about ourselves since our neighbor Gronk killed bigger wooly mammoths than we did.

EMBRACE WHO YOU ARE

This section might sound like that old *Saturday Night Live* skit with Stuart Smalley looking in the mirror saying positive things to himself: "I am good enough, I am smart enough, and dog-gone it, people like me!" However, there is one thing I have truly learned, which many people have said: Each person is unique and has a combination of attributes that make them special. No two people are alike.

Even if you share some characteristics with other people, you have your own experiences and path that have led to this moment. No one else has ever walked your path. The combination of your personality and your experiences, both good and bad, makes you unlike anyone else on the planet.

The challenge comes when our society pushes us to "fit in" and tells us that standing out or being different is bad. With my background in marine biology, I have studied a lot about fish. One of the most interesting behaviors of smaller fish is when they are schooling together. You might have seen times when a group of fish are swimming in a tight-knit ball, staying close to each other, with a predator circling around them. When the predator dives into the ball of fish, it is hoping to scoop up as many as possible.

But when you watch what happens in slow motion, you can see that because the predator cannot single out one individual target, it goes in with hope but usually comes out with an empty mouth. Then, every once in a while, one fish breaks the rules of the school, ends up on the outside, and then becomes an easy target singled out by the predator.

As we discussed in Chapter 3 about fears and the primitive parts of our brain, having a combined goal of being part of a tribe and surviving, most humans act the same way as schooling fish. Stay close, look the same, blend in, and stay safe.

Collectively, we are threatened by anyone who stands out from the crowd, "marches to a different drum," and doesn't do what the rest of the school/tribe do to blend in. I am not saying you have to go out and rebel, doing everything differently, but I share this because we are often taught to hide the things inside of us that make us special. And the feeling that society is judging us causes us to hesitate when it comes to being who we really are. (Spoiler alert: Always remember everyone has something going on, and truly, no one cares to judge you as much as you fear they are.)

STOP JUDGING WHO YOU AREN'T

Our society has a collective level of judgment of what people should and should not be doing with their lives. There is a generally accepted way of acting, or at least what is seen as the right path through life. It used to be referred to as the American Dream: graduate high school, go to college, get a stable job in your field, get married, buy a home, start a family, stay at your job or at least in your field until you retire, retire, enjoy your golden years, die. Some parts of that are still the norm and expectation, whether it's fair, appropriate, or even attainable. Then there is the whole "Keeping up with the Joneses" part that I won't even dive into. Suffice to say, expectations have always been a stressor on who we truly want to be, and social media has only magnified the appearance of the Joneses.

I have had a pretty winding path through my adult life. In my late thirties, I often met people who had degrees in the fields they actually worked in. No one ever said anything negative or judgmental about my path when I shared my history, but sometimes, I could see a glimmer of shock in their eyes. Even if they weren't judging me, it didn't matter because I judged myself for not following a straight path like them.

Then one day, as I was listening to a presentation, I realized everything I had gone through, building on my strengths and providing me with experiences (especially the tough times and rock bottoms) had molded me into the person I am. These experiences made me the type of person who understands hurt, pain, financial issues, success, adventures, new experiences, learning, and growing. That makes me the type of person who can speak with others and help them in different ways.

We were created to be different. We are not clones, like sea anemones. No one is exactly like anyone else, and no one has had the same experiences as anyone else. Your mom has been right all these years: You are special. The sooner you embrace your uniqueness and see it as an asset, the better off you will be when dealing with others.

FOCUS ON YOUR STRENGTHS

Here's the punchline: Always remember to focus on your strengths. Again, there are things that you know, have experienced, and were born with that define who you are in a way unlike anyone else. This means you also have a set of unique strengths. I am not going to say no one else has those same strengths . For example, I am really good at spreadsheets, data, and recalling stats and figures when needed. I'm good at consultative and in-vestigative sales and problem solving, and so on. None of those are unique on their own. However, when each of us combines our parts to become our complete and authentic self, that inter-section of all our strengths is both special and valuable to others.

In particular, because this book was written with the hesitant, or-der taker salesperson in mind, it's even more important to amass a list of your strengths in all categories, not just sales. If you are reading this book, hopefully, it's because your goal is to really embrace your sales role and find a way to be successful, even though you may not have thought of yourself as a salesperson in the traditional sense. And in my opinion, that is great because, to me, the world does not need more manipulative salespeople and sales tactics; it needs more people like you.

The best thing you can do for yourself is figure out who you are, what you are good at, and even more importantly, what you en-joy doing. There are things you do in which you can lose your-self—things that cause you to lose track of time, forget to eat or take a break, and shut out the rest of the world, leaving you in the "zone." If you are fortunate enough to have tried a variety of hobbies and activities and discovered what fits you best, congrat-ulations. That should be the number one item on your strengths list. Whatever fits you best is most likely at the crux of some per-sonal intersection of strengths, and hopefully, it is built upon the things you like to do and are good at. The one warning with this item is: Your passion has no business value unless someone will pay you for it.

If you have not found the thing you are truly passionate about, the thing that feels like the culmination of everything you are re-ally good at, do not worry. The best solution is always to try new activities. Try different creative projects, join various groups, keep exploring and looking for the thing that gets you excited.

Everything and anything can be classified as a strength, on the surface or at a deeper God-given talent level. Whatever that might look like. It could be public speaking, training, leadership, spreadsheets, analyzing data, researching, writing, hosting parties, entertaining, counseling, or coaching. There is an infinite number of strengths someone could have. To me, the purpose of life is to identify your strengths and put them to good use for the benefit of others.

The punch line was "Focus on your strengths." The question was actually "What is the first step to becoming self-aware?" To be aware of who you truly are is to embrace your strengths and your past, to know your passion and what you enjoy talking about or doing.

DON'T FORGET YOUR WEAKNESSES

I will not act like Mr. Positive by telling you how perfect you are, that you have no flaws, and that everything will be wonderful if you just focus on your strengths. If I did that, it would be a terrible disservice to you—filling you with a false sense of blind hope. Yes, life can be wonderful and great, especially when you maximize your strengths and focus on the positive.

At the same time, we all have weaknesses and flaws. No one is filled with only strengths, no matter how perfect their life might seem. Always remember that each person has two things: weaknesses and things in their past they really don't want people to know about. Your goal should be arriving at a place where you understand your weaknesses, come to terms with them, embrace them, and set them aside as much as possible.

Some books, trainers, and gurus will tell you to improve your weak areas. Some say to focus on your weaknesses and turn them into strengths. In my opinion, it all depends on what kind of weakness it is.

The three main categories in which we can be strong or weak are: skills, abilities (talents), and knowledge. Knowledge is the easiest one to improve because it is based on what you learn or experience. If you want to improve in this area, just read more, learn more, study more, and/or experience more things. The power of the internet has made gathering knowledge less valuable. Wisdom is more important. (I'll discuss why in the next chapter.)

Skills and abilities are a totally different matter. If your weakness is a lack of talent or skill, you might bring that up to a higher level of proficiency but potentially only to a point. Some people find it best to ignore their weaknesses and only focus on their strengths. For others, improving certain weaknesses is critical.

Like most people, I felt fear at the thought of public speaking and saw that fear as a weakness. I obtained my first professional sales position in 2002, via the residential mortgage industry, as a loan officer. By 2004, I was working with distressed homeowners who were on the path to foreclosure. To me, helping these people was more satisfying and felt like a better fit for who I was and what I cared about—helping people get out of trouble instead of helping people get into more debt. In 2006, I was working at a startup focused on helping people avoid foreclosure, and after a few months, I found myself running training sessions for new hires, which I had never done before.

I realized both training and sales are a form of public speaking, and when I was selling either face to face or over the phone, it was a presentation. And a presentation can be structured, built, and delivered similarly to a speech performed while standing in front of a room. The moment I realized this, I began what became a two-year journey with Toastmasters International. Toastmasters is a club that meets once a week where participants practice public speaking. For fun. Not via court order, or gunpoint, or blackmail. I voluntarily went almost every week for two years to practice and become proficient and comfortable with public speaking.

Usually, when I tell people about Toastmasters, they freak out. "Why on earth would you go do public speaking on purpose, for fun?" I will tell you, it might be one of the single most important things I ever did for my sales career, and I think if you are in sales, then Toastmasters will make a huge difference. Over those two years, I did dozens and dozens of speeches. This helped me become more comfortable with speaking, selling, and training.

At that point in my sales career, I felt like my selling abilities were decent, but I had a weakness—I was overly analytical, and always "in my head" when it came to getting comfortable in front of a group. I put in the effort to improve my public speaking skills, which then complemented the problem solving, training, and education abilities and talents I naturally possessed. Improving this area was well worth it.

STRENGTH EXERCISE

How well are you maximizing personal strengths in your sales career?

| Not sure what my strengths are | | | | | | | | | | Totally leveraging my strengths |
| 0 | 1 | 2 | 3 | 4 | 5 | 6 | 7 | 8 | 9 | 10 |

If you didn't rate yourself a 10, what can you use from this chapter to identify and focus on your strengths?

_____

_____

_____

_____

SUMMARY

The issue Ben faced was comparing himself to Carl (and anyone who was winning) instead of focusing on his own strengths and recognizing and embracing who he was, the uniqueness of his path, and the things that made him gifted in his own special way. As we sat there going through the exercise together, he realized he had several strengths, including the ability to ask pertinent questions, solve problems, and listen for what people said and didn't say that gave him clues as to how to help them. He didn't need to be pushy, or salesy, or trick people into buying. He didn't need to try to be anyone else. He just needed to relax, do what he was good at—that actually came to him pretty naturally—and then move people toward buying.

We all have strengths and weaknesses. When we go all in on our strengths, whether they are talents, abilities, skills, or even knowledge, we move closer to fully embracing who we are. No one else shares the intersection of experiences and talents that make you unique, just like no two people share the same finger-prints. There has never been another *you*, and there will never be anyone exactly like *you*. The key is to focus on your strengths, without judging them, and maximize what you are great at, the thing that causes you to lose track of time, and hopefully, is also something others will pay you to do. This is critical for creating authentic-based sales success.

Peter Parker's uncle told him (okay, Stan Lee wrote it), "With great power comes great responsibility," and in my experience, with great strengths comes the potential for great weaknesses. There are times when you can focus on your strengths so much that weaknesses become even more apparent, like when a brilliant scientist goes all in on their research and becomes even more introverted and socially anxious/awkward. A balance always exists between maximizing your strengths and improving your weaknesses as long as it is in alignment with achieving your *why*. Most of all, it is important to be as self-aware as possible. The more you know about yourself, who you are, what you like and don't like, and what you can do to help improve the lives of others, the happier and more fulfilled you will be. When you understand your fears and where they come from (Chapter 3) you can start to see who you truly are—that's self-awareness. Only when you are in alignment with your real self can you be authentic with others. And people might not act like it, but they crave your authenticity.

CHAPTER 6

AUTHENTIC SELLING TAKES LEADERSHIP

"The task of the leader is to get their people from where they are to where they have not been."

— Henry Kissinger

When Kevin was growing up, his dad was in the Army, and Kevin remembers feeling some pressure to follow in his father's footsteps. The pressure was even greater because his grandfather had also been in the Army. Kevin can still remember how proud his family was the moment he told them about enlisting. Four years later, he realized the Army wasn't for him, and he made the tough decision to leave the military despite knowing his father would be disappointed. After the Army, Kevin floated around in several companies, finally landing in a sales role that finally felt like the right fit. But he struggled to generate success, no doubt due to the voice in his head that told him he was a failure because he was not living up to the expected family legacy of military excellence and leadership. In his mind, he knew others saw sales as a sad option compared to the correct path.

As we grow up and experience more of the world, we find some level of self-awareness. At a minimum, we hopefully come to identify our fears. We also learn what motivates us and our *why* becomes clearer. But what most people don't realize is a successful sales career actually requires leadership skills.

In this last chapter of the Authentic section, we will explore the concept of leadership and how it is a necessary mental muscle to exercise to be successful in sales. And I am not just referring to "sales leadership," meaning a team leader or manager in charge of a sales team. I mean you, the salesperson, sitting at your desk making phone calls, standing on the car lot talking to people, knocking on doors, or meeting with prospects. The traits that make effective leaders are also the traits used by authentic, and consequently, effective, sales professionals. As you will hopefully see, it's your duty to be a leader to your prospects.

DEFINE A LEADER

Let's define a leader as someone who has commanding influence. Most of the time, we think of leaders as the people in charge of a team, group, company, or nation. In the military, leaders direct troops to complete an objective. True leadership is not about making people do things but rather inspiring them to follow. It's about persuasion, not manipulation. The U.S. military operates based on order following, which doesn't require influence. True leaders succeed through persuasion, not brute force or threatened punishment.

Leadership is a power that should be wielded carefully and with the right intentions. Charismatic leaders will get people to follow them, but the question is, "Where are they leading them?" When you lead from a place of improving the lives of others, then where you are headed is always going to be a better place.

Like any other skill, I believe leadership is a trait a person can develop and/or improve. Often people think we are either born leaders or born followers. This is not the case. If you fully embrace the traits that make someone a leader, you will become a good leader. It's important to keep in mind that leadership can also be situational. In some circumstances, you are the leader (at home, in the club you belong to, with an online community), and other times, you abdicate leadership to someone else, part or all of the time. This also means that, while you might not think of yourself as a leader in most areas, you can exercise that muscle as a salesperson.

PEOPLE WANT TO FOLLOW

In my opinion, most people are looking for someone to follow. Remembering back to the discussion about fears and our natural desire to stay in our comfort zone, we want leaders to show us it's safe to do that thing or go to that place. Ideally, we want to make the right decision in the quickest way possible as a result of being led. That is why so many get-rich-quick, lose-twenty-pounds-by-Monday, find-your-soul-mate-tonight salespeople do so well at selling their books, courses, seminars, or programs. People want to follow someone who will help them achieve their goals, and they are inspired by charismatic promoters who say all the right things. It's why a pastor with the right personality and gifts can motivate their congregation, with their message, hopefully but not always, in a positive direction.

One driver behind followers' actions is FOMO: Fear of Missing Out. People are especially susceptible to the leaders whom others around them are already following. Going back to our tribal days where lone individuals were tiger bait, we are hardwired to be part of the group—instinctually, we don't want to feel left out. A leader can reach a critical mass of followers where others don't even question joining their movement. Don't get me wrong; it's not always negative. There are great leaders, like Martin Luther King, Jr. and Nelson Mandela who inspire the masses to do better things for the world as a whole.

LEADERSHIP APPLIED TO SELLING

As a salesperson, the key to long-term success is inspiring your prospects to follow you. As a sales professional and leader, your goal is to protect your prospect—from high costs, low quality, loss of market share, etc.—shifting where they are now to where they could be with your product/service/help. You use persuasion to show prospects you're the leader they should follow (which we will cover in Section 2). When you do this at a pure level, your prospects feel inspired by your knowledge, expertise, ability, experience, and direction. They will want your product or service. They will believe in you and your company.

The greatest salespeople inspire others to follow their suggested directions. Most of the time, people attribute that to charisma. Of course, there are always smooth-talking, storytelling people who can get others to go along with them in the short term. But that isn't the only reason one will follow another, and that doesn't always work long-term. If you are like me, you might have enough experience with people who rely on charisma to know their intentions may be selfish, and overly charismatic tactics will actually trigger mental warning signals in prospective buyers.

It's important to mention again: With great leadership potential comes great responsibility. If we are going to change the way the world views sales professionals, selling your product or service should only be done with the good of those involved in mind and not for malicious, self-centered reasons. History has recorded countless leaders who inspired others to follow them in really bad directions. The sales profession has a negative reputation because of salespeople who used manipulation to make sales regardless of the buyer's needs—usually to meet the salesperson's selfish goals. My mission is to help you become part of changing that narrative.

AUTHENTIC SALES LEADERSHIP TRIANGLE

Countless combinations of traits are needed for a salesperson to operate as a leader, but three traits are mandatory to an authentic salesperson who wants to lead people to buying their product or service for the right reasons—wisdom, experience, empathy. Let's briefly look at each one.

Wisdom

Wisdom is applying the knowledge you have to effect a given situation in the best way possible. Information is great, and of course, very important, but, as an example, it is also very important to know the difference between a hammer, nail, and screwdriver and know that a hammer won't solve problems involving screws. As Miles Kington said, "Knowledge is knowing that a tomato is a fruit. Wisdom is knowing not to put it into a fruit salad."

To be genuinely skilled as a sales leader, you must have wisdom. Of course, you won't start out with much wisdom or even knowledge regarding your product or service. But the key is to gather as much information as possible as quickly as you can.

This is where the open and curious traits come in from Chapter 2. Once you fully understand your product/service, you need to learn about your prospect. Specifically, what types of problems do they have and what are their goals? Wisdom will allow you to apply the right tool (your product/service or better suggestion) to the prospect's situation.

Experience

If you pay attention, experience is a great teacher. Sales success comes from having knowledge and wisdom and being able to relate that knowledge and wisdom to the experiences you have had and your prospects' situation. You don't have to "walk a mile" in every prospect's shoes to be successful as a sales leader, but it definitely helps if you have walked enough miles to have seen how life works. Wisdom is applying your experience to the prospect's situation and coming up with a solution, even if your experience doesn't exactly fit the problem.

But keep in mind, if you have no experience with your prospect's problems, it will be tough to lead them at times. For example, if you have never struggled with alcohol addiction, you won't be a good AA sponsor. Here is where the power from being authentic comes into play. Your prospects will know if you have had similar experiences—good or bad, positive or painful. Be authentic with where you have been, and how your experiences can help you support them.

Another great way to gather experiences is to learn from others, especially your prospects. Once you have been in sales long enough, you will have seen countless scenarios you can draw from and share. And you can be equally great at leading through sales by combining what you have been through and all the stories you have heard from prospects.

To be clear, do not confuse experience with age. I am not saying you have to be a certain age to be a sales superstar. And I'm not saying you have to be married, divorced, a parent, or have gone through health or financial issues. I wouldn't wish unpleasant life experiences on anyone, and they are certainly not necessary to be successful in sales. However, I will say they do help a lot.

Empathy

The top of the triangle, the most important trait, is empathy. Empathy is the ability to understand what the other person is experiencing and wanting to help them get to a better state. The key is intentionally working for your prospect's benefit, not just your own. Great sales leaders make empathy a primary driver of their actions. When your goal in each interaction is to focus on the prospect's needs and provide them a potential solution, and you combine this attitude with your other sales leadership traits, you will win long term.

Empathy is a tricky one in sales. I have seen countless salespeople pretend to be empathetic to their prospects, only to bad-mouth them as soon as the meeting/call is over. If you don't actually care about your prospect's current situation enough to truly want to help them get to a better place, their long-term sales success will be tough to achieve. However, when you use authentic empathy, your prospects will feel it and want to follow your lead. We will expand on the value of caring about your prospects in Chapter 11.

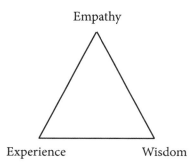

LEADERSHIP EXERCISE

How would you rate yourself in approaching your sales conversations as a leader to your prospects?

If you didn't rate yourself a 10, what can you use from this chapter to embrace your role as a leader?

_____

_____

_____

_____

_____

_____

_____

_____

_____

_____

SUMMARY

After reflecting on his heritage, Kevin realized he possessed the same leadership traits that made his dad and grandfather successful in the military. Instead of beating himself up over "just being a salesperson," he could now see how he was a sales professional *and* a leader. When going through the exercises to identify and embrace his leadership style and skills, he saw that the more he operated from the Leadership Triangle, the easier it was to meet his sales goals. Instead of leading people on the battlefield, he helped his prospects win their own wars and get to a better place.

After reading this chapter, you may be struggling to embrace the idea of yourself as a leader. Most salespeople who are failing to achieve their goals aren't fully embracing their leadership power as a vital step to achieve authentic sales success. That is why they end up on the order taker end of the spectrum. But, as I covered in this chapter, everyone can improve their leadership skills.

Leadership is all about inspiring others to follow you. If we extend the premise of leadership to your role as a salesperson, then your long-term success is predicated on your prospects following you "into battle"—not because you manipulated them, tricked them, or pushed them, but rather because you inspired them through your professionalism and expertise and authenticity. When you lead from a place of wisdom, experience, and empathy as a salesperson, your prospects will feel you want what's best for them. If you can also solve their problems or help them achieve their goals, you won't need to ask them to buy. Instead, they will ask you to let them be part of your "movement." And you will achieve great results as a sales professional.

What battle is your prospect waging? An eons-old war inside themselves that will first require you to show up as an authentic leader. Then it will take a very detailed understanding of how they think and a specific approach to helping them buy, which is where we are going in the next section. And you thought this was a simple sales book!

SECTION 2
POSITIVE PERSUASION

Now that you are aware of how important authenticity is in your selling role, we will continue to the second half of the Authentic Persuasion method. Being authentic is a necessary foundation, but it alone will not create a sales superstar. Without the goal of moving the sales process forward with persuasion, it is just a friendly, transparent conversation between two people—the kind you would have with your friends and family, or someone you just met at a party.

In this section, we will cover the action step part of your sales conversations by diving into persuasion.

The challenge I have seen hundreds of struggling reps face is that they do not understand the power of persuasion. They feel persuasion is a negative act done to control someone or trick them into doing what you want.

I am going to show you the formula for persuasion and how to use it. When done correctly, it is an amazingly powerful force for moving the right prospects forward. I am also going to cover how another profession uses a framework for their conversations that will work for you as well.

My goal for Section 2 is for you to believe in your power to persuade for the right reasons and to take a big step toward becoming a quota breaker.

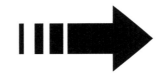

CHAPTER 7

USING THE POWER OF PERSUASION

"Your life does not get better by chance. It gets better by change."

— Jim Rohn

Samantha's sales struggles came from childhood experiences. As an only child, she had no choice but to tag along when her parents went shopping for major appliances, cars, etc. She didn't enjoy it, but even when she was older and could stay home, she didn't like being alone and bored. Consequently, she ended up sitting through many battles between her parents and salespeople.

Samantha specifically remembers times when salespeople really pushed her parents hard to buy using classic sales tactics. They would offer deals or say the item was the "last one" to create false urgency, and other salespeople or managers would be brought in to try to close the deal. Even as a kid, she could tell the process was wrong. Then, as an adult, Samantha found herself in sales, and she vowed she wouldn't do anything like what she had seen growing up. Her goal was to avoid pressure and tricks, yet she also found herself struggling to close enough deals to meet quota, let alone make the money she wanted.

Thus far, our journey has been about self-awareness, maximizing your strengths and focusing on *why* you are in sales, on the path to making the shift from order taker to quota breaker. In my experience, if you have the core traits for success as a salesperson, becoming a quota breaker is a matter of when, not if.

In this chapter, I want to start our discussion of persuasion by looking at the sales myths that give the industry, salespeople, and making money by selling such a bad reputation. I truly believe the world needs, wants, and deserves professional salespeople— so many good things happen as a result of a salesperson facilitating a transaction. However, that process has to be done the right way and for the right reasons. I don't want to dwell on the negative, but it is important to touch on the dark side of selling.

MANIPULATION VS. PERSUASION

Let's start by examining two words: manipulation and persuasion. For this discussion, we'll look at *psychological manipulation*, which is defined by Wikipedia as: "a type of social influence that aims to change the behavior or perception of others through abusive, deceptive, or underhanded tactics. By advancing the interests of the manipulator, often at another's expense, such methods could be considered exploitative, abusive, devious, and deceptive."

When a salesperson uses comments, questions, or other tactics to make a sale without regard for the buyer's needs, it is manipulation, especially if done in a deceptive way. Manipulative sales tactics and the subsequent ill will they generate have given the sales profession a bad reputation.

An example would be the term "snake oil salesman," which is based on traveling salespeople who went from town to town selling potions guaranteed to cure whatever ailed the buyer. These people moved a lot, whether their shop was set up in a wagon or moved into a storefront, because sooner or later, the townspeople realized the "magic" oil did not actually cure anything, and they ran the salesperson out of town, sometimes covered in tar and feathers.

The snake-oil salesperson repeated the cycle in the next town, using high pressure, false claims, and parlor tricks—often planting someone in the crowd with a fake ailment the potion would then "magically" or "scientifically" cure, depending on the pitch. Grand promises, tricks, and manipulation gave the illusion that the potion actually cured ailments. In the end, buyers bought empty promises and lies, and the salesperson profited.

Past manipulative sales tactics are responsible for how the world feels today about salespeople, especially by those who feel they are being taken advantage of. Why is that car salesperson so excited when you drive on the lot? Because you represent a new opportunity for them to sell a car and earn a commission. I am not saying salespeople shouldn't be excited to talk to new prospects or make money; I'm saying it's all about the underlying intentions. It's only a problem if the salesperson's winning means the buyer has to lose. Becoming this type of salesperson is what most well-intentioned people in sales are afraid of having happen to them, so they default to order taking.

If manipulation benefits the manipulator, what does persuasion do? *Merriam-Webster* defines persuade as: "to move by argument, entreaty, or expostulation to a belief, position, or course of action." Persuasion does not speak to motives, so it could be for either or all parties' benefit. To me, this means you can use persuasion for good or evil purposes—it is up to you.

Persuasion is open-ended, neither negative nor positive. When done right, persuasion benefits both parties and facilitates a win-win situation. It can, of course, also be used nefariously, just like manipulation, for the sole advantage of the one doing the persuading. I use the term "positive persuasion" to make it obvious what the intentions are of persuasion in sales. When you use positive persuasion, your goal is to help the other person get to a better place or state in their life or business.

WHY MANIPULATION WORKS

Fundamentally, if a strategy doesn't work, it dies out, right? Manipulative, deceptive selling has been around for a long time and still persists, so we know it works to some degree. Why does it work? Really, the question is: Why do people keep buying from salespeople and companies that use manipulation?

Psychologist George Simon outlines three requirements for successful manipulation: 1) hiding aggressive intentions and behaviors while being friendly/pleasant, 2) knowing the psychological vulnerabilities of the other person and determining the best tactics to use, and 3) having no issue with causing harm to the other person.

To clarify and expand those points, the psychological manipulator is one who has no problem with causing harm to someone else for their own benefit and leveraging the other person's weaknesses and insecurities, all with a smile on their face. There is a long list of tactics that may be employed, ranging from lying, rationalizing, evasion, and diversion, to guilt trips, shaming, obfuscation, and playing the victim.

Here is a summary of a partial list of reasons people are susceptible to manipulation taken from Martin Kantor's book *The Psychopathology of Everyday Life: How to Deal with Manipulative People*:

- Dependence: Emotionally dependent people need constant reassurance that they are loved, making them vulnerable to those who portrays themselves as caring.

- Naiveté: If the person is immature or naïve, they tend to believe exaggerated claims.

- Impressionability: Someone who doesn't look at statements critically can be easily seduced by charmers.

- Honesty: Honest, trusting people often assume others are equally honest and trustworthy.

- Altruism: Altruistic people can be targets because they might be too honest, fair, and empathetic.

- Carelessness: People who are careless and do not pay attention usually don't get enough information before making decisions.

- Loneliness: If someone is lonely, they are susceptible to anyone who pays attention to them.

- Materialism: Materialistic or greedy people are likely to fall for get-rich-quick schemes.

- Frugality: On the other end, frugal people have a hard time saying no if they see something as a bargain.

- Narcissism: Narcissistic people are easily manipulated through flattery.

WHAT PEOPLE REALLY WANT

The success of snake oil sales was predicated on knowing when people were catching on that the products didn't work and moving far enough away to get ahead of their reputation. Attempts by companies and individuals to use manipulation have always existed—advertisements, sales presentations—but it fails when the public becomes educated. Now, in the age of connectedness and instant information, it is much harder for salespeople with bad intentions to exist in business long term. Yet, there are still people manipulating others and making money from it.

What do people really want? This is where it gets tough because, theoretically, people want honesty in advertising and sales. Reading through the list above, we see a wide range of people with many different needs and motivators, but they usually want something that fills a need, emotionally or physically, and caters to deeper psychological triggers they aren't even aware of, which take control of their buying decisions. Yet it can be tough to be "good" when it comes to selling. A lot of evidence, such as rich salespeople and "successful" companies, support the idea that using manipulative sales tactics truly works. But long term, they don't.

What people really crave most is honesty and authenticity. Most people want to have someone listen to them and care about their needs and wants. Tim Sanders talks about it in his book *Love Is the Killer App*, where he asserts that nice, smart people succeed in sales and business, defying the common wisdom that it takes cutthroat, self-centeredness to win. Deep down inside, people truly want to deal with someone they can trust. While some might fall for manipulation tactics, what they really want is to be persuaded.

PERSUASION EXERCISE

This one can be tough, but how would you rate yourself on using persuasion versus manipulation?

If you didn't rate yourself a 10, what can you use from this chapter to understand and use persuasion?

_____

_____

_____

_____

_____

_____

_____

_____

_____

_____

SUMMARY

After I shared with Samantha the differences between manipulation and persuasion, and we identified how she could use her strengths to sell in line with what people wanted, she could clearly see a path to succeed in sales. She identified where she saw manipulation used when she was growing up and why it truly felt wrong to her, even as a child. She had vowed not to cross that line to get the sale, and she was excited to learn fundamental ways to achieve her financial goals while helping her prospects get what they wanted and needed.

Throughout history, there have been people who used manipulation to get others to do what they wanted, whether as a sales tactic in business or in relationships. We know manipulation works despite our theoretical aversion to being manipulated. Yet here we are, in a world full of salespeople, organizations, and advertisers using various forms of manipulation to get what they want. This has also caused most buyers to be cautious or defensive, and for many people in sales to hold back from fear of making sales in the wrong way.

While doing the right thing and following the Golden Rule are great strategies for how to conduct yourself, feeling good about yourself because you've done the right thing is hopefully the best reason to be honest and above board. In the information age, the speed at which information travels and the level of transparency the internet and media provide seem to be making it harder and harder to manipulate consumers for forever.

Long term, the truth always comes out. There are fewer and fewer places to hide. Companies like Wells Fargo (with its corporate-wide account opening scandal) and Volkswagen (with its worldwide emissions fraud scandal) are reeling from the instant and widespread damage to their reputations in the wake of intentional deceit. Doing the right thing is not just the right thing to do; it is the best long-term strategy for success.

Note, not all consumers are making better decisions, which is why at times government has to step in to create more business, marketing, and compliance-related regulations. Again, this is why I see it as your duty to help people make good purchasing decisions. If you aren't successful in persuading them, they could end up going down the street or calling someone else who might not have the best intentions. Again, this is why I feel it is your duty to use positive persuasion.

Now that we have the manipulation discussion out of the way, it's time to understand why it can be so challenging to get people to make decisions. In Chapter 3, we spent time unpacking your fears and how they hold you back. In the next chapter, we will discuss ways the primal part of your prospect's brain keeps them from buying from you and what you need to do about it.

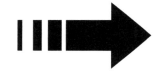

CHAPTER 8

BUYING SOMETHING NEW = CHANGE

"It is not the strongest of the species that survives, nor the most intelligent that survives. It is the one that is most adaptable to change."

— Charles Darwin

Amy did everything her manager taught her, yet she still wasn't getting the results she wanted. When she spoke with her prospects, it was clear to her that the best thing for them, and not just for her and her commission, was to sign up for her company's service. It was obvious to Amy that she could help them, and she tried to lead them to the finish line. While her prospects had financial goals, usually centered on retirement or buying a home, they weren't taking action. Amy knew her company's service could help prospects meet their goals, but people kept telling her no. Most of the time, she heard, "We need to think about it," which gave her some hope that they would sign up later. But most of them disappeared, never to be heard from again.

Thus far, we have focused on you, the salesperson—your goals, your reasons for being in sales, your fears, and your challenges. Now we turn our attention to the prospect. In particular, we are going to explore what they are afraid of. As we have discussed, everyone has fears. Some people are better than others at taking action or making decisions anyway, but some level of fear exists in each person.

When a perfectly qualified prospect doesn't buy your product or service, especially when there is a clear benefit for them, then fear is paralyzing them. And it's not just any fear; it is the fear of change.

In this chapter, we will look at how the fear of change drives your prospects' actions. Then we will cover what you can do to help them move forward in the face of fear. My goal is to help you see that your job as a sales professional is to move each prospect past their fear of change and to buy from you for the right reasons. Persuading past this mental barrier is an important part of becoming a quota breaker.

YOUR PROSPECTS' ANIMAL BRAIN (FEAR RECAP)

Remember earlier we discussed the animalistic, primal part of our brain that is focused on survival? In certain parts of our minds, the only goal is to survive long enough to ensure our DNA continues on. Because of this inherent survival trait, most people fear change. Again, something "different" back in our cave-dwelling days could have been fatal. Our brains are trained to see danger and not always opportunities.

For example, thanks to the governments in most First World countries, food has to be tested, certified, and labeled as safe for consumption. Yet people still don't like trying new things or eating foods they aren't familiar with, despite the fact that they logically know it's okay. It's not dangerous, just different, and the fear generating part of our mind is so strong at times.

Of course, fear varies for each person and is situational. Some people are deathly afraid of spiders, heights, clowns, snakes, and so on, while other people are totally fine jumping out of an airplane, yet fear public speaking, dogs, or spreadsheets.

What are your prospects afraid of? That is the million-dollar question. Each one will be afraid of something different, but it's safe to assume they all fear change, and buying from you equals a scary change. Of course, there are the fearless prospects who accept the "risk" and take action anyway. Those are the ones who buy easily, the "early adopters" who have a high tolerance for change, are excited about new things, and don't need a lot of convincing.

WHY WOULD THEY CHANGE?

The most important question is: Why would your prospects want to say yes to change? (And, of course, this applies to anyone, not just your potential customers.) There are two main reasons people decide to change: fear of pain or hope for gain. Let's look at each.

Fear of Pain

Avoiding something painful has been shown to be a way stronger motivating factor for people's actions than the positive end of the spectrum. That is why the "stick" is usually more effective than the "carrot." Again, you can thank our primal brain trained over centuries to avoid anything that could cause pain. I know I keep bringing it up, but it is key for understanding why people do or don't do things—way back in the day, death was right around the corner if you ate rotten meat or broke a leg. There was no doctor or medicine like there is now, and those scenarios could lead to a slow, painful death.

Our mind is designed to keep us safe. Safety requires avoiding pain. Often, doing nothing is perceived as the better choice (again see Chapter 3 about the Comfort Zone)—until you are faced with something painful and must act. That trend builds over time to a point where the person needs either to do something different or face death.

This is usually referred to as "rock bottom," where someone hits their breaking point and finally stops the bad decision cycle and makes a change. You see this situation happen with addicts, people dealing with financial troubles, and those in abusive relationships. Unfortunately, two things are true with hitting rock bottom: everyone's bottom is different, and not everyone will hit it and then to take different action.

One way to motivate your prospects forward is to help them realize the pain of their current situation or where they are headed if they don't change direction. It is, of course, simple when their decisions are causing an unbearable situation and you can provide a solution. If they aren't in pain, but on the path to it, it is still possible to sell them a solution for the issue you see them headed for. That is a little tougher; it takes more persuasion to help them visualize their painful future and then provide them with a better path. The skill you will need in each situation will depend on your prospect's pain tolerance, and whether it is a bruise, a cut, or a gunshot wound type of issue.

Hope for Gain

In an ideal world, people would be motivated by the hope for gain. They would work hard and want to make changes because they wanted to get to a better place with respect to their health, finances, relationships, career, etc. Do you want to get into better physical shape or lose weight so you can feel better? Do you want to create financial security to live a more comfortable life? Do you want to find the perfect mate so you can live happily ever after? These should be the stronger motivators and drivers of action, right?

Most people's instinctive minds are not motivated by gain. Now, of course, whole industries are built around feeding into the basic areas people want to improve. There are companies and individuals with get-[fill in the blank]-quick programs for people to become wealthy and retire, lose weight easily, get that beach body before summer, or find the perfect relationship.

The challenge with the "carrot" is that the individual needs to have a reason why the carrot would drive them. In the same way that you, the salesperson, have to have a *why* to motivate and drive you to succeed, there must be a reason to go for the gain. Otherwise, it will be just as easy to stay comfortable and safe. Aiming for gain comes with the risk of failing and ending up back in the comfort zone, or maybe even in a worse spot, which is the scenario our mind constantly shows us. For most people, it's safer (and way easier) to stay where they are than to try to improve.

FACILITATING CHANGE

Remember the discussion about schooling fish staying together so they don't get singled out and eaten? Our animal brains think the same way: *There is safety in numbers, so don't stand out.* Being odd could equal death. If you want your prospects to make a change and buy your product/service/idea, show them that others are doing it. If someone else has bought it, or eaten here, or traveled there, or jumped off it, then this proof gives a level of assurance that we will also be okay. Testimonials act as social proof, which is why they are so powerful as one of the oldest sales strategies around.

One reason eBay became so popular was it had a ranking and review system for buyers and sellers—helping both sides reduce the fear that comes from online transactions. It's the same reason a lot of people rely on the Better Business Bureau to validate a company they want to do business with. It's why I know I am not alone in scrolling straight to the bottom to read Amazon product reviews from other people who bought the item I'm looking at. (Is it safe or did they die? Okay, maybe not die but feel upset?

Angry? Embarrassed?) Referrals are so powerful in overcoming this fear (more on this in Chapter 20) because they are firsthand testimonials from people who saw a movie or ate at a restaurant or got a massage or bought a house and had a great experience (the opposite of harm or embarrassment your prospect is worried about).

In sales conversations, I suggest using stories of how you helped a third party in a similar situation. These are not random tales of people you sold to, but stories about people the prospect can identify with, people who were in a similar situation. For example, if you are a real estate agent and meet with a married couple who are expecting their first child and looking to buy a home but are nervous about the process, you might mention you worked with another couple who had a newborn, and they were very excited because owning a home meant they could raise their daughter in a home long term, and the house they picked also had room for a second child. This home would be the place of years and years of memories for this blossoming family. The key with this type of conversation is that it be accurate, specific, and relative to your prospect. Over time, you want to amass lots and lots of stories you can use in future conversations.

Another key to helping people overcome the "change" hesitation is to offset the risk associated with the purchase. If you are trying to get someone to buy paper towels, there is very little risk (although, fascinatingly enough, if we really dive deeply into brand loyalty, we see it is the result of the same fear of change, safety in the "known," animal brain tendencies, so many people will tend to select their usual brand whether it's a car or toothpaste). Why do people love Apple products so much? Are Apple products the best? No, not in all ways. But people feel safe buying what's familiar to them. Because they know what they will get; they will have a fairly consistent, expected experience. It's the same reason most people frequent chain restaurants or stores. I have been to Starbucks in dozens of cities around the world, and I know what I will get, with little risk of buying something I have never had before and being unhappy with it. It is also common to see Americans travel to other countries but still eat at familiar chain restaurants. It's a safe haven in an unfamiliar place.

But if you are working with someone who wants to buy a $30,000 car, more potential risk exists than picking out toothpaste, especially if the person has small reserves of cash with which to recover from a loss if they make the wrong choice. Car manufacturers and salespeople offset that risk by offering five-year warranties, free oil changes and service, loaner cars, and even seven-day return options—some allow you to bring the car back and get a full refund if you are not happy with it in the first week. Those types of offerings have become more and more standard and go a long way toward easing the minds of prospective buyers, especially if they have never bought your brand before.

Whatever you are selling, do your best to understand the "risks" the prospective buyer is taking, whether real or perceived. In your conversations, be prepared to address those risks if they come up. You want to know all the weaknesses of your product or service (and yes, despite what every founder thinks, all products/services have a downside, big or small). Be prepared for all the objections your prospects will throw at you.

The third suggested strategy is to help your potential buyers make the move to the new product/service the safer option by seeing the risk of staying where they are. If you can make your product/service into the best option, it will reduce the risk. Your goal should be to get the risk down to zero by highlighting their current situation's downside. Stay in a burning building or trust me enough to grab my hand to escape? Make the right choice that clear to your prospects and you will persuade more people to buy.

I could imagine that our lucky ancestors might have had a cozy shelter with fertile hunting groups nearby. Life wasn't terrible, yet there was Fear Of Missing Out (FOMO) that there could be a better place. But, in life, there are also no guarantees that a different location will improve life. Everything seemed okay until food sources started to dwindle, and they thought maybe another place could be better. Yet they decided to stay put. Still, as their local food options got worse, leaving to find another location actually becomes a lower-risk activity than staying. So *safe region one* just became *dangerous and unpredictable region one*, meaning that *unknown area two* is now a better option.

When selling, it's important to determine if the prospect's current situation is bad in regard to their short and/or long-term goals, and if so, how bad. If you can find and highlight how your product, service, or idea is the hands-down safer, smarter choice, it will be much easier to make the sale.

CHANGE EXERCISE

How would you rate your ability to recognize each prospect's fear and use your sales process to get them past it?

If you didn't rate yourself a 10, what can you use from this chapter to help your prospects embrace change?

_____

_____

_____

_____

SUMMARY

What Amy was missing from her sales process was the act of helping her prospects overcome their own barriers to change. When she heard the dreaded "I need to think about it" from her prospects, she could now see she had failed them. She had not fully done her job as a sales professional to help them see the path ahead was indeed safe. She had not shown them the pain they could be avoiding or the gains they could be achieving. What she blamed on "bad leads" was, in fact, mostly her lack of skills in getting them to embrace change. She let her prospects stay in their comfort zones, which equaled a lot of non-sales.

I know it might seem like a lot of pressure, and a potentially difficult task, but if you are selling anything, you are up against tens of thousands of years of survival instincts residing in each person, whether they are conscious of it or not. Of course, not everyone is the same, and you will encounter people who seem completely okay with change and do not hesitate to make a purchasing decision. On one hand, don't take it personally when someone says no to what you are selling because, most likely, they don't even fully understand why they are saying no—it's all instinct. On the other hand, take it completely personally because it also means you failed to help overcome their fear of change, and thus, are not living up to your duty as a sales professional.

With this quick lesson on deep survival instincts, you can approach your sale from a different perspective. Your goal should be to make the buying decision as "safe" as possible. Sharing testimonials from other people who purchased and lived to tell about it is a great start and the basis of online review and feedback sites. Knowing that people will default to playing it safe, remember always to have options ready to help offset the risks they feel. Gail Sheehy said it best: *"If we don't change, we don't grow. If we don't grow, we aren't really living."*

Now that you understand what your prospects fear most and some ways to help them take action anyway, it's time to start building our persuasion process. The main requirement to persuasion is trust. Creating a level of trust takes several steps. In the next chapter, we will start with the first one: building rapport.

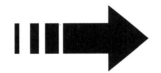

CHAPTER 9

BUILDING RAPPORT FOR THE RIGHT REASONS

"People will forget what you said, people will forget what you did, but people will never forget how you made them feel."

— Maya Angelou

Sara had the gift of gab. She could talk to anyone about anything no matter the topic. People had told her for years she should be in sales. Unfortunately, after taking the leap, she was unable to get consistent (and commission-worthy) results. Her prospects told her how much they enjoyed talking with her; some would even thank her for being so nice even if they didn't buy from her. The ones who did move forward always gave her perfect survey responses. If sales were a popularity contest, she would have won big and been cashing giant commission checks. Yet she was barely making quota most weeks and didn't know what was missing.

Have you had this experience? Do you feel like you have amazingly effortless conversations with most of your prospects, where time seems to fly by, only to have them say no in the end? Have you been told the key to sales is to build rapport—get them to like you first? People like to buy from someone they like, right?

In previous chapters, we outlined the prerequisites for making yourself into a sales professional. So far we have covered fears, both yours and your prospects. Ultimately, it really does come down to one factor: trust. In the last chapter, we covered how some people have a very low tolerance for fear related to change, and most of your prospects will need to feel like they can trust you and your company before they will buy.

In this chapter, we will begin to cover the foundations of persuasion so you can go from order taker to quota breaker. You cannot just tell your prospects to trust you because everyone knows that when someone says you can trust them, it usually means the exact opposite. The path to a trusting relationship begins with rapport. Believe it or not, there are right and wrong ways to handle the rapport-building stage.

FOR THE RIGHT REASONS

Rapport is an important step in interacting with people. Fundamentally, as the saying goes, people are more likely to do business with people they like. Creating a healthy rapport at the start of a new relationship is a requirement.

As with most things, the primary factor for success is your intention behind what you do, so why you build rapport is even more critical than how you do it. Looking at manipulative salespeople we don't enjoy interacting with, we can picture them doing their "rapport steps" because they know it's important to get close to us. Maybe it includes lots of over the top flattery, insincere compliments, and grandiose promises about having exactly what you need. But the intention behind it is personal gain only. And you can sense it.

One example that always sticks in my mind comes from when I was training to do Business to Business (B2B) sales that involved meeting a prospect in their office. The instructions were, upon entering the prospect's office, to look around quickly to find something that indicated a hobby or passion, and then start talking about that one thing. Don't get me wrong. I don't think that is a negative way to act. Again, it comes down to the intention and sincerity behind it. Are you actually interested in the other person and excited to find common ground? Do you actually care about their fishing trip, family, or golf game? Or do you do it just as a necessary step to advance the conversation and, ultimately, get what you want—a sale?

If you don't care about sports, awards, cars, or whatever they are interested in, are you asking them about it for your own selfish gain? At the end of the conversation or transaction, it will all come down to your intentions—your gain, their gain, or mutual gain.

NOT NERVOUS/STALLING

One sign of an order taker, or just an insecure salesperson, is the use of rapport to stall the sales process. They try to avoid the tough parts of the conversation that could trigger confrontation or rejection, like the need for sensitive information or moving toward the close. Of course, there are always chatty prospects who just want to talk and make it tough to control the conversation. But it is another thing when you avoid controlling the conversation and spend most of the time socializing because it's easier.

Several reasons exist for not nervously stalling in the rapport step. The first is that time is money. Of course, we all know that, and as a sales professional, hopefully, you understand that well, but most order takers I have worked with do not value their time. And, even more importantly, do not value their prospect's time. Sharing recipes, talking about last night's big game, discussing politics, or just chit-chatting takes up precious time. If you broke your income goals down to how much you would make per minute, would you spend so much on unnecessary small talk?

You need to find a balance between rapport that supports conversation and builds trust and rapport that wastes time. While your time is precious, you never know how much time your prospect has to speak with you, whether it's on the phone or face to face. It is important always to assume that at any moment the prospect will need to end the conversation. Their child could start crying and need them, someone else could call them with something more urgent than your conversation, their phone battery could die, or their boss could walk in and demand their attention. Always ask yourself, "What if the conversation ended right now? Would I have enough information or did I provide enough value to make this sale on the next call?"

The third reason to avoid nervous stalling during rapport building is that it will subconsciously cause your prospect to distrust you. Similar to how animals can sense fear, most people pick up on cues indicating when someone is nervous. This will then signal that the chatty person rambling on and on is worried about something, maybe potential information they don't want you to know about, and is thus trying to suppress it. If you find yourself spending a lot of time on rapport, talking about light and easy topics, or making long-winded, one-sided statements, ask yourself, "Am I doing this because I'm worried about them finding something out about me, my product/service, or company that could make them distrust me or become disinterested?"

NO DANCING

While it might not fall under the rapport category, it is important to discuss how these nervous, stalling monologues can show up and potentially kill your chances of closing the sale. I call it "dancing," and you want to avoid it at all costs.

Here is a scenario you have likely either done yourself or witnessed: A prospect asks a question somewhere on the spectrum between curiosity and out-right-deal-breaker-objection. In response, the salesperson goes into a long-winded monologue that may start with a response to the question/issue, but then diverts into all kinds of directions.

Here is what it would sound like:

Prospect: Is there a fee for this?

Salesperson: Yes, there is a fee, but don't worry about that. By the way, we have been in business for five years, and we have a good rating with the BBB. You can check that out on our website and see that we have helped thousands of people. If you want, I can send you the links for that and some testimonials we have....

I have seen sales reps who will rattle on way too long in response to a question. Why does this happen? Fear of either not knowing the answer or fear the prospect won't like the answer, leading to a lost sale, so the salesperson tries to distract them with "verbal dancing." They are dancing around the topic, but never really addressing it in a succinct way. For most people, this isn't a premeditated tactic; the reaction is mostly unconscious, and comes from the hope that if you say enough things, a) the other person will forget what they asked, and/or b) will hear something they like in everything thrown at them and thus be pacified enough to move forward with the conversation and transaction, thus repairing trust or rapport that might be in question.

Save your dancing for the club. When your prospect asks a question, just answer it.

If you realize you do this, it's important to identify why: Lack of confidence? Lack of knowledge? Lack of trust or faith in your product/service/company?

Then it should be your mission to increase your confidence, knowledge, and/or trust. If you can't, that's your cue to find a new company or career.

TALKING RATIO FOR SUCCESS

With rapport, you need balance. You don't want to jump straight into business during the conversation and make your prospects feel like they are dealing with the DMV. But you need to modulate how much rapport you want to build while not spending too much time chit-chatting (time you may or may not have). What is the right ratio?

Whether it's building rapport, answering questions, or just filling out the paperwork to conclude the sale, for most interactions, the best ratio is one to two—you speak about one-third of the time and your prospect speaks two-thirds. Of course, during a demo or sales presentation, you will do most of the talking; however, before and after, the prospect should do two-thirds of the talking.

Why that specific ratio? Two reasons: First, as my grandma used to say, "You have two ears and one mouth, so listen twice as much as you speak!" (I think this is great advice in general, and most people definitely do not follow it enough.) The second is a quote credited to Theodore Roosevelt, "People don't care how much you know until they know how much you care!"

When we combine those two, we can see the psychological basis for the one-third/two-thirds ratio. Most people will subconsciously and consciously feel that someone who listens to them cares about them.

Your prospects feel the same way. If your sales style is lots of self-promoting monologues and long-winded answers, they will assume you don't care about them. If, instead, you let them talk most of the time and actively listen, they will get a deeper sense that you do care.

ACTIVE LISTENING

This is where Active Listening comes in—actually listening intently when someone else is talking. We all know what the opposite looks, feels, and sounds like. As you are speaking, you can tell the other person isn't listening, and instead, is probably thinking about what they want to say as soon as you stop talking. They might even cut you off because they can't wait to talk.

You know they are not listening and that almost nothing you say will matter. They won't be able to give you any time, attention, or empathy because they are truly stuck in their own head, in their own world.

Unfortunately, I suspect this has been an eternal human trait. Maybe it is because people don't feel *heard* enough at home, so they instinctively try to talk more and louder to get some attention. I am not going to blame social media, but since it could be amplifying the issue because it involves no direct, personal interaction, the art and skill of unselfishly listening to another person is not a requirement.

I think the world needs more active listening combined with empathy. When you are actively listening, it comes from a place of caring for another, whether they are a stranger, your server at a restaurant, your best friend, a coworker, or a family member.

BUILDING RAPPORT THROUGH LISTENING

When it comes to sales, it is even more important to listen actively and intently. Remember, rapport is all about building the foundation for a trusting relationship. The goal of your rapport step, upfront and all throughout your conversation, is really to ensure the prospect feels heard and cared about. Actively listening is the key to more and higher quality sales. Where do salespeople get into trouble when it comes to listening? In my experience, salespeople, especially new ones, are concerned about what to say next and having the right response ready so they don't lose the deal. When a prospect is talking, most salespeople hear the first part of the sentence and then start formulating their response, just waiting for the prospect to stop talking. It could also be that the salesperson is so structured and/or rigid that they cannot go with the flow of the conversation or that they have a need to be in control by always thinking, planning, and plotting what they need to do next in what they view as a "chess match." They think, as a salesperson, it is a competition *against* the prospect, not a collaboration *with* or *for* the prospect.

How do you combat the tendency not to listen to the prospect? First, know your stuff and be okay not knowing all the answers to all possible questions. On one end, learn everything you can about your product/service so you have your mental knowledge base filled and ready to go at will. Also, know the best answers to common questions prospects will ask. These two categories should, at some point, be memorized so you do not need to think about them in advance to recall and share with the prospect. At the same time, you want to be okay with not knowing things your prospect might ask about.

The second way to increase listening effectiveness is to totally let go of worrying about what you are going to say at any moment. Your goal should be to have a conversation that is both completely free-flowing and, ultimately, follows your sales success formula roadmap. You want to plan to the highest level possible in your sales process, operate at the ground level, and adapt to whatever comes up. Your goal is to have conversations that moves with the same ease as a professional performer onstage doing improv based on random topics from the crowd and turning it into spontaneous gold.

For order takers and new reps, one of the biggest challenges is doing everything that needs to be done at once: talking, typing, taking notes, reading a script, running a demo, calculating figures, and using a CRM. Usually, the part that gets left out when the rep is overwhelmed in the heat of the moment is listening to what the prospect says. However, your number one key to sales success is getting to a place as quickly as possible where everything on your list becomes automatic. All your processes and scripting are on autopilot. At that point, you can just focus on the other person and have a conversation between two humans.

RAPPORT EXERCISE

Most people think they are good at building rapport. How would you rate your ability to do it in a productive way?

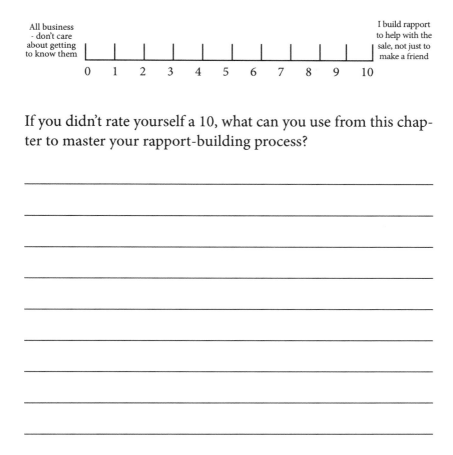

If you didn't rate yourself a 10, what can you use from this chapter to master your rapport-building process?

_____

_____

_____

_____

_____

_____

_____

_____

_____

SUMMARY

By going through the rapport exercise and stepping back to analyze her conversations, Sara could see she was leaning on the rapport-building, chatting portion of her sales conversations and hoping that if her prospects liked her enough, they would buy from her. Of course, some of her prospects did, but most did not. While her intentions was always good, her challenge was to limit the time she spent talking and instead spend more time listening. She also needed to focus more on actually moving toward the sale instead of just being a friendly order taker. She was missing the important part of building rapport: building it and then moving forward. She was afraid of being "all business" because she didn't like when salespeople did that to her. She genuinely liked people and wanted them to be happy. The key to her sales success was realizing she could help prospects feel good at the beginning (rapport building), pleased throughout (maintaining the rapport during the conversation), and, ultimately, satisfied when purchasing from her.

The rapport step usually comes at the conversation's beginning, but it is also valuable throughout the interaction with prospects (and people in general). Some scenarios could warrant warming things up with chit-chat and then diving 100 percent into business—think about a doctor with a good bedside manner. Most times, sprinkling rapport at the beginning and end of the selling process is valuable. Remember, it is possible to mess up rapport building if you are not careful.

The main key is to ensure your intentions are good, whether in creating rapport or in life in general. When your heart is in the right place, what you do will translate effectively long-term. Just make sure you see rapport as a stage in the sales conversation, not the primary goal. Always remember that at any moment your prospect could need to end the conversation, so balance your relationship-building efforts with moving the process forward.

In *How to Win Friends and Influence People*, Dale Carnegie listed one way to win friends is to be a good listener and get others to talk about themselves. When in doubt, talk less, ask more questions, and listen. Your goal should be to have your prospects speak most of the time. This will help them feel like you care, with the important side benefit of also providing you with lots of key information to help your persuasion process. In the next chapter, we will continue building the trust portion with why questions are so critical and how to ask them the right way.

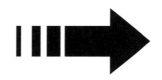

CHAPTER 10

ASKING QUESTIONS

*"The important thing is not to stop questioning;
curiosity has its own reason for existing."*

— Albert Einstein

Bill had only been in the sales game for a year. He liked helping people, but he struggled to consistently do well. Some weeks, everything seemed to flow and he closed sales easily, but other weeks, he couldn't make anything happen no matter how many calls he made. *I am doing the rapport part correctly*, he thought to himself. *Maybe I am just unlucky.* He watched other reps crush their quota week after week with ease, but he didn't know what he was missing. He was following the script, going through the process—what he didn't have was enough information about his customers.

In the last chapter, we talked about building rapport as a critical step; however, that is just a starting point, not a final destination for closing deals. What Bill was missing was the questioning part of the conversation. Many reps I speak with don't believe me when I tell them how powerful asking questions is.

When you ask questions, what value could that provide? How can questions tell you something you don't already know based on all your experience selling? Why does it matter what someone's goals are or what they are afraid of? In this chapter, we will cover why questions are so important and the valuable insight the answers provide you with.

WHY QUESTIONS ARE KEY

Let's start with the most obvious reason for asking questions—to get answers. It's why you ask your children, your significant other, and your coworker questions. There is something you want to know, or do not understand (mystery), so you ask questions, and hopefully, get an answer. The catch in asking questions is that the whole process relies on trust. To get the other person to answer with truthful and valuable information, they have to trust you enough to answer. Now, of course, it is a spectrum where one end is questions that rely very little on trust (What is your favorite color? How is your day? Do you like broccoli?), and on the other end, questions requiring complete trust (What is your biggest fear? Will you marry me?). One important rule with asking questions is to ensure you have built a trusting atmosphere in the relationship that gives you permission to ask questions that will require that level of trust. That is why it is important to start with rapport before moving forward in your sales process.

If one goal of asking questions is to get information, then what types of questions should you be asking? That depends on what you're selling and how much information you need to help the person decide to buy, which is where order takers stop short. Remember, we discussed in Chapter 6 that people prefer to "buy" instead of being "sold." Really, the goal with questions is to find out why that person would want to buy. And as we will discuss in Chapter 12 the key is uncovering a problem they need/want to solve.

Like a detective, lawyer, or doctor, you ask questions to uncover pain, problems, and truths. In my experience, there is always some level of pain or problem the prospect wants to resolve. Don't believe me? Why does someone want to buy a new cell phone? An obvious problem could be that their phone broke and they need a replacement right away. Or maybe the battery life has become terrible and they can't go very far from their charger or it will die. But what if they have a perfectly good phone and they are waiting outside the store for the latest upgrade—what pain/issue would buying a new phone solve? One answer could be FOMO—Fear of Missing Out—they don't want to feel "left out," uncool, or behind the technological times relative to the people they know.

GOAL OF QUESTIONS

The primary goal of questions is to uncover *their* potential need or desire for your product/service. The better your questions, the more value the answers will have. The answers are what you are looking for, and they allow you to tailor the sales conversation to provide the exact solution, if it exists, to their issue.

The second reason for asking questions is to make the other person feel better—specifically about you. When you use Active Listening (see Chapter 9), it builds trust. By asking questions, actually listening, making physical or mental notes, and referencing what they said, you show that you actually care about them. You ask questions that ultimately uncover their problems, needs, and desires. You ask questions to be able to offer a solution based on their needs. How do you build trust? Start with rapport, ask questions and listen, and then empathize with them (see Chapter 11). Trust will be built following that process without ever having to ask for it.

The third reason to ask questions is human dynamics—people like talking about themselves, telling their stories. I mentioned in the previous chapter that, fundamentally, people feel good when they are doing the talking, and it usually builds a more positive feeling toward the person listening. Your goal in sales should be to ask questions to get the other person to talk. If you find you are doing most of the talking—going from salesy sales pitch monologue to monologue—then you will potentially show the other person that you care more about yourself than them.

The driving force behind your questions should be a deep level of empathetic curiosity. The most successful salespeople I have ever encountered are deeply curious about other people and the world in general. They want to know as much as they can about whatever is in front of them. When I am in front of a prospective buyer, I go into hyper-detective/doctor/lawyer mode. My goal is to find out the deepest information I can to help solve their issues—fear, pain, hardship, goals, whatever it is that drives them. My goal is to ask until I can answer the question: What wakes you up at two in the morning in a cold sweat? Always remember, the bigger or deeper the issue or pain you can help someone overcome, the bigger the rewards will be (and that does not always mean financial).

THE ONE WHO ASKS THE QUESTIONS....

Have you ever watched a movie or TV show with courtroom scenes? Each time, there comes a point when a witness on the stand gets pummeled with questions. The questions usually start out easy and nice to warm up the witness, but then get harder and harder.

Yes, the attorney is trying to get to the root of the matter at hand. But more importantly, the attorney's goal is to stay in control. Fundamentally, in any conversation, the person asking the questions is in control of the conversation. And in those courtroom dramas, the attorney is in total control of the situations via asking questions, and the witness is more or less a punching bag being verbally knocked around by the attorney.

If you want to be seen as a professional or an authority figure, it comes down to being the one primarily asking questions, especially in a sales situation. The person asking questions is in charge.

If you find yourself on the receiving end of questions, you have given up control of the situation. For order takers, that could mean certain sales death.

The key is to be conscious of when you are not in control. If you have lost control and are afraid to get it back or don't know how, we will discuss what to do in Chapter 12. If, however the prospect is wrestling for control and you intentionally allow it, that's another matter.

As we discussed in Chapter 8, part of your prospect's mind is afraid of change, wants to stay in their comfort zone, and is fighting for control of anything it can. During your sales interactions, that scared part wants control and tries to get it by asking questions. It is important that you walk the fine line of answering the questions and providing comfort to that fear while not letting it win the battle. At times, you want to let go of control in the conversation. When you do so with intention and then take back control when necessary, you will achieve greater results.

AVOIDING THE THIRD DEGREE

Remember when you were a kid and your parents would ask you about your day? You would share a little but didn't really feel like talking about it all. Or maybe something embarrassing happened, so you didn't want to share. Now, remember when you were a teenager and you would come home late, or get a bad grade, or start hanging out with a certain new girl/boy. What did your parents do? They asked question after question. It felt more like you were being interrogated under a bright light for a crime you didn't commit. You just wanted it to stop, but your parents always seemed to want to know more, and more, and more, and more.

After reading the first part of this chapter, you might think I want you to barrage your prospects with questions, but that is not the case. Many salespeople worry in advance about asking too many questions from fear of upsetting the prospect. A fine balance exists between interrogation and useful discovery of information to determine if you are selling what your prospect needs.

How do you help your prospects feel like your goal is to learn information to help you help them rather than feel like you are digging too deeply, getting too personal, or trying to uncover some tidbit you can use against them? That is where empathy comes in. You are asking questions because you care. You want to know so you can help. I have always achieved better results with less resistance when I let the prospect know my intentions and the why behind the questions I will be asking. "I have been doing this for a while, and based on my experience, not everyone is a good fit for our product/service, so I want to ask you some questions to determine if this would make sense for you. I don't want to waste your time if this isn't what you need."

That type of statement will go a long way toward the prospect understanding you are asking questions to be of better service to them, not to upset them. Figure out the best setup comment you can use to help your prospects understand why you are about to ask them questions. If you tell them the *why* in advance, they are more likely to answer. If you can help them see that your goal as a professional is to help, you will close more deals.

FIFTEEN-MINUTE DOCTOR APPOINTMENT

In my training, I use the example of a doctor visit a lot because I think it is one of the best examples of questions (and an assumptive sale/close—see Chapter 13) done right. If you can replicate what a doctor does during their visits with patients, you will win long term as a sales consultant.

Let's look at how a doctor visit goes. You sit in the little room waiting for the doctor to come in, after the nurse took some vitals, weighed you, and measured your height. Then the doctor arrives, looks at your chart for a brief second, and starts asking questions. Questions about why you are there, where it hurts, or what you are struggling with.

Then they start putting you through the paces of more poking, prodding, measuring, and assessing, with more pointed questions like "Does it hurt when I push here?" and "When you do this, how does it feel?" This could go on for five or fifteen minutes. At the end of their examination, the doctor writes some notes, and then shares their diagnosis, if they have one. If they don't know enough, they will order more tests to determine an accurate diagnosis. If they have determined what it will take to get you into a better place, they will give you a prescription and instructions for things to do and/or avoid. In the final step, the doctor asks if you have any questions before sending you on your way with an action plan.

Modeling yourself after this process is a very effective way to operate as a sales professional. No long monologues at the beginning. No getting battered with questions and objections from your prospects until you determine if you can really help them. It's just about you being in control and asking questions until you can give them a proper diagnosis and prescription, which we will cover in the next chapter. Most order takers feel weird asking questions and controlling the conversation. But when you act like a doctor, you will find greater success, and your prospects will appreciate it.

RATING YOUR QUESTION SKILLS

Rate your effectiveness for asking questions, and getting answers.

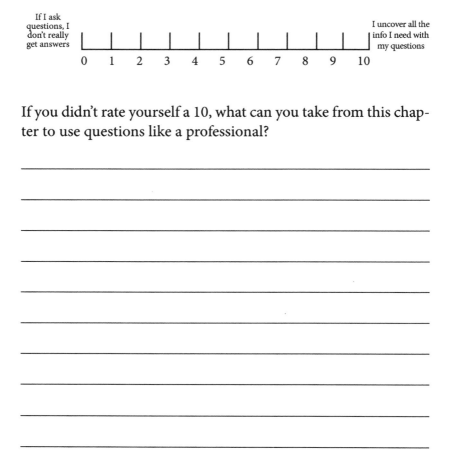

If I ask questions, I don't really get answers

I uncover all the info I need with my questions

0 1 2 3 4 5 6 7 8 9 10

If you didn't rate yourself a 10, what can you take from this chapter to use questions like a professional?

_____

_____

_____

_____

_____

_____

_____

_____

_____

SUMMARY

Bill felt that asking too many questions would upset his prospects. He didn't want to make them feel like he was probing too deeply. But he realized he didn't really know if they would truly benefit from what he sold or how it would specifically help them. This meant he couldn't give customized suggestions that would address each prospect's deeper needs. Bill hesitated to ask questions because he felt it was intrusive. Then he learned that prefacing his questions by telling people why he wanted more information allowed him to take more control of the conversation like a doctor would. He could then dig until he got enough information. This was the part he was missing, keeping him from producing consistent, great results in sales.

The key to success in almost everything comes from the questions you ask, and the information it uncovers. These questions can help you get to the heart of the other person's pain or issue, whether they were consciously aware of those parts or not. The questions can also help you show the other person how much you care about them by offering them something special—listening and waiting to know the answers.

Questions can also be a way to guide and control the conversation to help your prospects get in a position to buy what you are selling. Always remember, the person asking the questions is in control. At times, you might lose control, and it's important to be able to recognize that and regain control when needed. You will struggle to achieve long-term success without using questions and controlling the process.

No matter what you are asking, if you don't know why they want or need to buy from you, it will be tough to create consistent, high-level sales results. Imagine a doctor who doesn't know why someone needs treatment. They wouldn't have too much success getting patients to follow their directions. When you use curiosity from a place of empathy, you will achieve sales superstar status. Questions are a powerful force, so before continuing with how to use them, we have to address where empathy fits into the sales success formula.

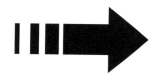

CHAPTER 11

EMPATHIZING FOR SUCCESS

"I follow three rules: Do the right thing, do the best you can, and always show people you care."

— Lou Holtz

When John started his first "real" sales job, he was asked to shadow Trevor, seasoned sales veteran, and learn from him. Trevor just gave off a "sales" vibe. He taught John about the product they were selling and the pricing, but what he conveyed most was his strategy: "Find 'em, fleece 'em, forget 'em!" Trevor's strategy was all about finding a prospect, doing and saying whatever it took to get them to spend as much as possible (earning Trevor the maximum commission on each deal), and then moving on while hoping they didn't call back to complain. John thought it seemed the wrong approach, but knowing no other way, he tried to copy Trevor.

The number of times I have heard Trevor's sentiment used by someone in sales is disheartening. If you spend enough time on the sales floor, you get conditioned to that type of attitude. If you are a paying customer on the other end of this mode, you remember such interactions, and often, extrapolate that feeling to all salespeople. Trevor's kind of attitude is pretty terrible and leaves people thinking all salespeople are just looking to separate prospects from their money.

In the last chapter, we covered the topic of questions. This was just an overview for the importance of them within the sales process, plus how order takers stumble in that category. We will dive deeper into questions and the doctor analogy in the following chapter, but I feel it necessary to fill in the final part of the trust formula—empathy—before we go any further.

In this chapter, of course, I am going to argue for why it's your duty to take a different sales approach. Deep down, we are all the same; we want the same basic things, hope for the same things, and are afraid of the same things. What the world needs more of is caring, so my mission is to help empower you to infuse sales with caring. If you are operating like an order taker, you might already think you care about your prospects, which is why you don't push them to buy. But success can be created by combining caring about your prospect's future with helping them take action.

SHOULD YOU CARE?

"Should I really care about my prospects?" is the fundamental question. The answer is really easy—it's the right (and profitable) thing to do. We know doing the right thing is always the way to go. Caring about someone else and putting their needs ahead of your own goals is the best strategy if you want long-term success in sales and in life.

Sure, you can throw consideration for the other person out the window and sell lots of things that aren't a great fit to people who don't really need them and won't really use them at an inflated price. You could use a manipulative, uncaring approach and make a pile of money. We all know businesses and salespeople who use this model. And, at times, it seems like they are successful, that no one seems to notice, but when you aren't actually doing the right thing for people, eventually, the good times come to an end.

When you care about your prospect's wellbeing, you will likely tell the truth in your sales process and your answers to their questions. It's a cliché but very true that it's always easier to remember the truth. An even cheesier, true cliché is: The truth will set you free. When you come from a place of caring about the other person, and thus, giving them true and accurate information, if they do not want to buy your product/service, you know at least you did the right thing, told them the truth, and did your part to make the world a little better place.

USING EMPATHY

Before we move forward, I want to explain what I mean by caring. I am referring to being empathetic. According to Dictionary. com, empathy is "the ability to understand and share the feelings of another." I have always translated that into a three-stage process: 1) actively listening to the other person, 2) discovering what issue, problem, struggle, or goal challenges them, and 3) caring about their long-term success in a way that may mean telling them things they don't always want to hear—giving them the truth in a kind, loving way.

To me, caring for another person is about giving them information, advice, or direction that will get them where they want to be, even when you know it might not be easy, and they might not enjoy what they hear. To get to that point in a conversation takes a base level of trust, or it will not be received well. But building a deeper level of trust takes expressing greater empathy. It's a loop that should feed itself.

An example we can all relate to is getting children to brush their teeth. Our goal as a parent is to get the child to: a) brush their teeth daily, and b) develop a good habit that lasts a lifetime so they will have healthy, strong teeth and gums. To a kid, being told to brush their teeth feels like parents nagging and making them do something unfun. Parents can see the long-term benefit, but kids don't want to hear it. You care about them, but they resist the truth. If they trust you enough, they will do it anyway.

As a consultative, problem-solving, sales professional, you can see what your prospect might not regarding their own situation. Most people struggle with seeing the right solutions or how to get to a better place financially, health-wise, in relationships, and mentally. But you can see it from the outside, and once you understand their situation through the questions you ask, you know the right path for them (whether it's with your product/service or not). Empathy is the desire to help them get to that better place for their benefit, not just yours.

DOWNSIDE AND UPSIDE OF CARING

Is caring always the best strategy? Yes. Does it always result in a sale? No. Caring about the other person, to me, is always the correct approach. But there are a few things to be aware of. The first is that often you will tell people the truth or provide advice with regard to your product/service/idea and they won't like what you tell them. Sometimes, that will make them happy; sometimes, that will make them upset with you. Think about what happens when a close friend is making poor decisions and you try to help them by giving advice. Sometimes, it goes well; other times, they don't want to hear it. But because you care, you want what's best for them.

Most people decide to buy based on emotions, and then they look for justification intellectually that it's the right choice. Here is where researching, reading reviews, and talking to a salesperson comes in (and potentially triggers analysis paralysis, like we will discuss in Chapter 13). These are all strategies to prove what they "want" to buy is a good decision. If your suggestions aren't in line with what the person thinks they need, even if the person is wrong, they could be disappointed or even unhappy with you. You become the naysayer who didn't facilitate their emotional purchase—just like your friend who gets angry when you point out how they keep dating the same type of jerk over and over again.

Also be aware that another downside of caring is that the assumptive closes we will cover later, based on your assessment and empathy for their situation, could make you come across like a pushy salesperson. Your prospects could question your intentions in a "What's in it for you if I buy?" kind of way when you give them a strong recommendation. I have had many prospects question my motives for pushing them forward, I have to explain to them it's because I care and can see how they will benefit.

If there is a downside to caring, of course there is also an upside. When done correctly with empathy, the prospect will appreciate it, even if they don't fully recognize that it is present. Deep down, they will be glad you told them the truth. It can also yield longer-term results (see Chapter 20: Generating Referrals).

It seems silly to say, but the other good reason to care about your prospects and their long-term wellbeing is that it solves the "How do you sleep at night as a salesperson?" question. I bring up this point with anyone looking to get into sales who has had their own negative experiences with salespeople. They worry about what they will have to do to close deals (manipulation) and are afraid of how they will feel as a result (dirty, guilty, wrong). When you come from a place of caring, using empathy to power your sales focus, you will never have to worry about the propriety of the deals you close. This is why caring is a vital part of this persuasion section. Even if you have to use a strong persuasive approach, you will still know you did it for the right reasons.

KEY TO WINNING BY CARING

The tough part for salespeople can be justifying an empathetic and caring approach to managers/owners. When you care about the best interests of your prospects, and aren't trying to manipulate them into buying anyway, there are times it will not result in a sale. (See Chapter 19 about telling the wrong buyers no). I recommend using one word—abundance. I know that might seem like a buzzword at times, especially in a Law of Attraction, *The Power of Positive Thinking, The*

Secret kind of way. Whether you believe in those things or not, it is fundamentally true—there really is more than enough for everyone.

My personal, guiding principle when it comes to selling or enrolling anyone into anything comes from Zig Ziglar: "You will get all you want in life if you help enough other people get what they want." Ziglar doesn't say, "Take yours first so that you can have everything you want," and he doesn't say, "Get everyone to buy what you are selling so you can have everything you want." Rather, Ziglar speaks from a place of abundance. When your focus is helping other people get what they want or need, over time, eventually, you will get the things you want. And not some things—all the things.

When you come from an internal belief focused on abundance, you know that whether or not the person across from you buys does not determine your long-term success. If you care about people and look out for their best interests ahead of your own, giving them buying advice, direction, and information that fits their goals, needs, and desires, then you may or may not make the sale, but you will be on the path to long-term success and many more sales. Either way, you did the right thing. And if you remember there are more than enough people out there to sell your product/service/idea to, then you won't worry about manipulating people to buy your stuff.

If you are ever challenged by this concept, I suggest you put things into perspective with a little math. I once helped a company sell its SaaS platform (Software as a Service) to the SMB (Small and Medium Business) market. To help the team, I did the math with them. There are currently 30.2 million small businesses (less than 500 employees). The goal of each sales rep was to close 20 deals per month, or 240 deals per year. Over a 10-year career that works out to 2,400 closed sales. That number might seem like a lot, but to put it into perspective, those 2,400 deals represent 0.00795 percent (2,400/30.2 million)—less than one-one hundredth of a percent. Even if fifty reps were on the team, in ten years it would still only be 0.397 percent (not even half of one percent) of the potential customer base.

CARING EXERCISE

How well do you embrace/trust in abundance?

I only focus on commissions/ deals

I care about my prospect's wellbeing

0   1   2   3   4   5   6   7   8   9   10

If you did not score yourself a 10, what can you do to shift your mindset around abundance? (And, you can also do the math calculations—see below for instructions.)

_____

_____

_____

_____

_____

_____

_____

_____

_____

_____

As an extra credit exercise, let's do some math. (Yes, I know you thought you wouldn't have to do math.) How big is your customer *universe*? [*Universe* is a marketing team used to describe the total number of potential prospects for a business.] Next, how many deals do you need to close per week, month, quarter, and year to achieve your income goals? Now imagine you are in your role for ten years, so multiply your yearly customer number by ten. Last, divide that number by your company's total prospect universe. If that number is less than 0.01 percent (my guess is it's a fraction of a percent), then you can easily trust in abundance!

SUMMARY

When John realized what he was being taught did not line up with his own personal philosophy of how to treat people, he took a different approach. He focused on caring about each person and facilitating sales that would get them to the best place possible—for them, not him. He leveraged the power of abundance and was able to close more sales than some of his "hardcore" sales coworkers who were just trying to make money any way they could. John learned a few lessons about caring the hard way. The main one was that caring is not the same as being passive. John had to find the balance between giving someone a virtual hug because he cared and getting them to take action.

Empathy and caring are truly things the world needs more of. If you find yourself further at the order taker end of the spectrum because of your concern for how other people feel. I want to embrace the true power in that. My goal is to empower you to succeed by defying the normal sales conventions, and actually help people. If you get nothing else out of this whole book, I hope you get that it is okay—actually critical—to care about the person across from you or on the other end of the phone. Remember that we are all the same inside. We all have fears and challenges, hopes and dreams, a past and a future. And that prospect is coming to you with the desire to deal with a professional they can trust.

Caring and doing what is right isn't always easy, especially finding the right balance of caring and wanting the best for someone while pushing to make it happen. As a sales professional, you have to see what the person could or should do and then move the conversation toward the sale. The key is to do it for their reasons, with the right intentions, and for the right prospects who should buy your product/service.

Lastly, we can't discuss empathy without a reminder that everyone is going through something. And by something, I mean pain, hardship, struggle, difficult situations, or tough decisions— *life*. Life is happening to everyone, and most people keep their struggles to themselves. Each person you come across every day is struggling with something. They could have recently lost a loved one, ended a relationship, lost their job, or be struggling with health issues or how to pay their bills. When you make that realization, it will change how you approach people.

Order takers are usually skilled at empathy. They care, which is why they don't push. But from a place of empathy, it's actually your duty to help that qualified prospect buy from you. Using empathy instead of judgment, you can apply your question-asking strategy to uncover the other person's painful parts to help solve them, whether it is with your product or service, or just by listening to and being there for them in those moments. In the next chapter, we will go back to our question-asking discussion to provide a framework for turning that empathy into success, for taking the trust that has been created and producing new customers.

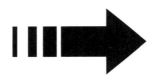

CHAPTER 12

DIAGNOSING, THEN PRESCRIBING

"I solemnly pledge to dedicate my life to the service of humanity; The health and well-being of my patient will be my first consideration; I will respect the autonomy and dignity of my patient; I will maintain the utmost respect for human life...."

— Excerpt from the Hippocratic Oath

Chris was actually really good at asking questions. His conversations flowed well as he moved in and out of the rapport-building stage. He had learned the company's sales system well. But as you have probably guessed, I wouldn't be mentioning him if he had achieved sales superstar status. He asked his prospects the questions; they answered. He pushed them forward to buy; they resisted, saying they needed to "think about it." He got frustrated; they never called back. He felt like he was following his training, all the prescribed steps, and, of course, it was working for some of the other reps, but most of his sales coworkers weren't winning either. Chris started to think maybe the company's sales process was the problem. Yet I observed that Chris wasn't connecting what the prospect was saying to how he could help.

Before our important discussion about empathy, we were focusing on the questions you should be asking and why. But asking the right questions is not enough to ensure success, especially for sales professionals at the wrong end of the order taker-quota breaker continuum. Knowing you should ask questions and which questions to ask is very different from actually doing it correctly. So what is the *correct* way?

In this chapter, we will take the conversation about questions to the next level. The key focus should be to understand how to effectively ask questions and listen to the answers so you can achieve sales success. It's one thing to ask questions, checking boxes off on your mental or physical sales process checklist; it's another to actually take the information (both answers and non-answers are valuable) and respond appropriately. At some point, you must listen to what your prospect says, then step forward with the best solution.

GETTING TO THE ROOT OF PROSPECTS' PAIN/GOALS

As I have mentioned several times, a vital key to success, including the use of questions, is intent. What is the actual goal behind your questions? What information are you hoping to get? What will you do with that information? What data is needed to do your job successfully? You need to know the answers to these questions before you can succeed with asking your questions.

Most reps struggling to create consistent success—whether new to sales and overwhelmed with everything they have to know, say, and do, or experienced and set in their ways—are probably not asking questions with the proper intent. They are asking them to get them over with and move on. This may be because you don't know what to do with the answers or you already think you know what the prospect should do and why.

Your line of questioning should be meant to dig and probe until you find the root of the prospect's goals and desires or fears, pains, and issues. What are they dealing with mentally, and can you help them get to a better place? If you are in sales but cannot answer the question, "Why should this prospect buy my product/ service?" then you are not a salesperson; you are an order taker. Order takers aren't usually asking questions so they can understand the situation and use the information intelligently in their closing strategy. They are doing it because they were told to. Like doctors, professional salespeople use questions to uncover the real issue and then focus on solving it. In fact, there are a lot of parallels between highly effective sales professionals and doctors.

WHAT IS MALPRACTICE?

There are good and bad doctors out there, just like there are good and bad salespeople (and good and bad examples within any profession). Good doctors ask questions, examine patients, run tests, and pull from their knowledge of symptoms and solutions. They are open to researching to find answers And they might even consult other doctors who might have the key to helping the patient. Bad doctors see a patient, and instead of really listening to them, feel like they already have the solution. Maybe they are inappropriately motivated by commissions or kickbacks from pharmaceutical or medical supply companies. They end up prescribing the same types of medications or run the same tests no matter what the patient is saying. They don't see the patient as a person with a unique experience and issue, but more like a means to an end.

What happens when a doctor does something that harms the patient? Sometimes it results in some kind of malpractice inquiry. In the United States, and probably most places in the world, there is an expectation, based on the doctor's medical training, certification by medical boards, and the Hippocratic oath doctors take, that a doctor will be competent.

Historically, there has never been a sales university or certification program. I recently discovered there are actually accredited colleges offering degrees in sales, but as of this book's printing, there is no nationwide sales effectiveness and ethics governing body to ensure salespeople have been educated and trained to do the best they can for each prospect. They aren't certified, regulated, or even insured in the event of causing harm. And there is definitely no oath salespeople must take before picking up a phone, knocking on a door, or speaking with someone who walks into the store or onto the lot.

In the absence of a certification program, how do you avoid selling malpractice? First, follow this underlying principle: *Prescription before diagnosis is malpractice*. This is important to memorize and also have mentally ready to tell a prospect.

If your doctor immediately jumped to a solution and gave you a prescription or wanted to send you for surgery without going through their diagnostic due diligence completely, and they turned out to be wrong, it would be malpractice. If they follow the correct process and are still wrong, then they most likely won't be liable because they can show that they made an informed decision. This is why *prescription before diagnosis is malpractice*. The doctor must diagnose before prescribing the solution, or they fail to uphold their professional duty.

AVOIDING SALES MALPRACTICE

How does this relate to sales? Let me give you an example from my time as a mortgage loan officer. In 2003, real estate was approaching a feverish level where it felt like everyone was rushing to buy a home or investment property. It also felt like everywhere you looked, there were ads for bigger loans and lower interest rates. Prospective borrowers were focused solely on interest rates, and the first question out of their mouths when they called me was, "What is your interest rate?" A lot of people were rate shopping because residential mortgages had become a commodity. And when you are involved with commodities, you know the buyer is only looking at key factors—in this case, the interest rate and fees.

When buying a home, the interest rate is particular to the borrower based on many factors, such as credit score and history, loan to value ratio (loan amount compared to property value), debt to income ratio, and income and asset documentation. When loan officers throw out interest rates without gathering data first, the quoted rate is a shot in the dark. It's like a patient calling the doctor, telling them what's wrong, and asking for a specific drug—based on an ad they saw on television. If the doctor gave them that prescription, it would be malpractice. It's the same with throwing out interest rates, usually low ones, to keep the prospective borrower on the phone.

In sales, this situation is usually referred to as a "bait and switch," but in reality, it is sales malpractice. The rate, fee, and term might be available for certain people—the few who meet the requirements in small print. I started telling prospects that we couldn't provide them with a rate prior to asking questions and pulling a credit report. If they got upset, I would say that prescription before diagnosis is malpractice, and I wouldn't give them an uneducated quote just to earn their business, knowing that down the road, I would have to provide them a more accurate and probably higher rate based on their specific information. As a direct result of sales malpractice in the mortgage industry, over time, regulations came out requiring certain disclosures when providing rate and fee quotes.

It can also be construed as sales malpractice when you feel pressured by your prospect to answer their questions. I am assuming your organization offers multiple solutions. To tell a prospect a price without complete information about their needs and qualifications is sales malpractice. Don't do it, and don't feel pressured into breaking that practice and oath to yourself.

PLAYING DOCTOR EXERCISE

How would you rate your ability to use questions to diagnose, prior to giving your sales "prescription"?

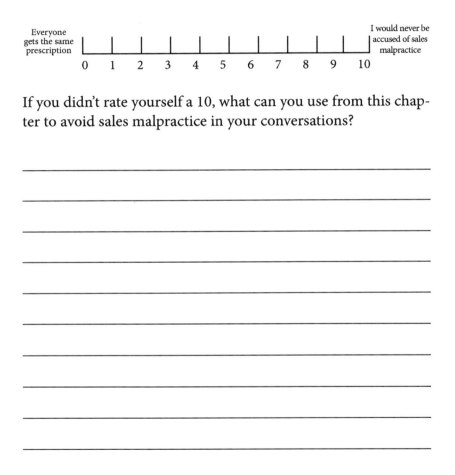

If you didn't rate yourself a 10, what can you use from this chapter to avoid sales malpractice in your conversations?

_____

_____

_____

_____

_____

_____

_____

_____

_____

SUMMARY

It turned out that Chris' issue was that he wasn't truly listening. He had the rapport and questioning steps down—during calls you could hear what seemed to be his perfect execution of the company's sales process—but when the prospect answered his questions, he wouldn't seem to react or ask a deeper follow-up question. If they offered information he hadn't asked for, he would gloss over it and just keep moving forward rather than use it to help him better serve the prospect. Because Chris' intent was completing the process, and not ensuring the best outcome, he never really dug deeply enough to uncover what the prospect really wanted or needed. He was basically a question-asking order taker—and he had a record of poor sales to show for it. And he never took the conversation forward to a diagnosis based on the answers.

Many people "played doctor" as children, diagnosing and treating their siblings, stuffed animals, parents, or anyone they could find. Whether you played doctor or not, if your goal is to be a sales professional, remember you can learn a lot from how doctors function. One important rule to always remember is to avoid a sales malpractice lawsuit. It is critical that you live by the philosophy: *Prescription before diagnosis is malpractice.* Don't give out solutions until you have the information you require.

At times, prospects will pressure you to jump straight into the price, fee, rate, etc. You are the professional, similar to the doctor, so do not give in to that pressure. It would be better to have them walk away because you wouldn't want to give them an instant quote with a figure you know you'll have to change later. (Trust me, the prospect will be very unhappy with you down the road if this happens.)

Remember to use active listening in your process. This takes preparation. Learn what you need to learn, prepare what you need to mentally prepare, and memorize what you need to be able to share. Have this all on recall in your mind so when the prospect is talking, you don't have to think about what you will say next. Your ultimate goal of having successful, empathetic conversations is to let go of worry about what your responses will be and just go with the flow.

Doctors who are ineffective in their process fail to persuade. When they don't perform with rapport, empathy, and question steps, and don't listen to the patient's answers, they don't build trust. As a result, the patient could want a "second opinion." Have you ever disagreed with a doctor's diagnosis/prescription or known someone who asked for a second opinion? It's because the doctor didn't follow the persuasion process and fully build trust prior to providing the prescription.

When you listen, you learn details about the other person. When you learn, you can then solve. When you solve, you will make sales. When you make sales, you will be a sales superstar. In the next chapter, you will learn what to do once you know your prospect's prescription.

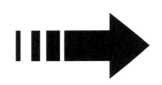

CHAPTER 13

ASSUMING FOR THE RIGHT REASONS

"Successful people are always looking for opportunities to help others. Unsuccessful people are always asking, 'What's in it for me?'"

— Brian Tracy

Jason liked to research and understand all the options available in any situation. He didn't need to be an expert at everything, but he definitely wanted to be prepared for most questions that could come up. He also felt it was his duty to provide lots of options so the prospect had all the information and could make their best decision. As a consumer, his walls went up and he ran the other way whenever he was dealing with a commission-hungry salesperson who was trying to steer him toward what they wanted to sell and not what he wanted or needed. It shocked him when, as a salesperson, he gave people multiple options, and they still didn't buy from him. He wasn't doing as well as others and was desperate to figure out why.

Okay, this time I am referring to myself. I used to make many assumptions that negatively affected my sales success. In this chapter, I will share which assumptions to avoid and why. I will also cover which ones are vital to a successful sales career. The key is using them as a tool—they have great power when used correctly.

My grandma always warned me against making assumptions about someone or something. "Squirt," she would say (she called me Squirt my whole life), "when you make an assumption, you make an 'ass' out of 'you' and 'umption'!" We all know that assuming is bad, but when it comes to sales, there is actually value in assuming certain things about your prospects. To perform as a sales professional, and not an order taker, requires making assumptions as a critical tool in the positive persuasion toolbox.

DON'T PREJUDGE

Let's start with what not to do when it comes to assuming: prejudging. Prejudging in sales is making a decision or judgment about your prospect based on incomplete information. The classic example of sales prejudgment is when a new prospect walks onto the lot or into the store wearing dirty, ratty clothes and the rep makes a decision based on their appearance about their financial situation. It can also happen over the phone when a rep makes snap judgments based on the language a prospect uses or their accent.

Why is this so wrong? Put simply, when you judge someone based on initial impressions and incomplete information, you will be wrong a certain percentage of the time. Not all the time—there will be times when you are spot on with your mental assessment. (See *Blink* by Malcolm Gladwell for a fascinating biological basis for the accuracy of snap decisions.) This judgment usually comes from years of experience and your filter, view, and bias of the world. If you see someone with dirty, torn clothes and an overall unkempt look walk into your dealership, you might assume they aren't a legitimate, qualified buyer.

The challenge is more about the times when you are wrong. The worst that can happen with spending time on someone you could have prejudged but didn't is that you waste some time you could have been spent on someone else. But if you dismiss the prospect too soon, and were wrong about their ability to buy, you potentially miss a sales opportunity. We have all heard stories of the person who walks into the car dealership and no one wants to talk to them because they look homeless. All the seasoned salespeople ignore them, yet there is that new, hungry rep who doesn't "know better" and isn't "too busy" who shows them some vehicles, treating them like anyone else. Then it turns out the person came to buy and had the cash to purchase on the spot.

No matter how much experience you have in sales, don't prejudge a prospect based on appearance or first impressions. Despite all the times you might be right, the times when you are wrong will be very costly to both you and the company you work for. The main suggestion I have for all salespeople is to: a) stop prejudging, and then b) ask your pre-qualification questions quickly and efficiently to determine if they are a qualified prospect you should continue spending time with. You want to balance wasting your time with bad prospects by giving everyone enough of a chance to determine who will be a potential sale. Don't pass up potential opportunities because of snap judgments.

ANALYSIS PARALYSIS

We need to take one more human behavior diversion to cover why it's important during your sales process to assume. Our free will loving side needs the feeling of having choices, but our brain craves to keep us safe while preferring simplicity. Analysis paralysis is a term used for when our mind gets overwhelmed with choices. *Wikipedia* describes it best: "Analysis paralysis (or paralysis by analysis) describes an individual or group process when overanalyzing or overthinking a situation can cause forward motion or decision-making to become 'paralyzed', meaning that no solution or course of action is decided upon." The end result is the state of doing nothing instead of making a decision, usually as the result of too many options, too much research, and/or too much analysis. Thus, the term analysis paralysis.

What does it sound like when a prospect has gone into analysis paralysis? You will hear comments like, "There are so many choices; I don't know which one to pick," or "I need to think about it," or "Let me do some research, and I will get back to you." If your prospect says *research* or *options,* they might have mentally fallen into analysis paralysis, and, you will have a hard time closing that deal.

What causes this analysis paralysis in a sales situation? For most people, it can be caused by the prospect's pursuit of the perfect, right, and/or safe decision combined with too many options. If you have ever been to a Cheesecake Factory restaurant, you know exactly how this happens. Their menu is twenty-one pages long and has over 250 items to choose from. Even when you successfully narrow down your focus to one category of food (burgers, salad, seafood), you still have an overwhelming number of choices. I have been there enough times to see other people struggle to choose, usually only doing so under the pressure of the server's fourth visit to the table.

Too many choices can be a bad thing, but why? Don't we like choices? Don't we like the feeling of "freedom" to choose? Yes and no. We want the illusion of choice, but what most people really want is the "right" choice. The issue with choice, once again, goes back to our primal brains. Many people, especially those with analytical personalities, fear making a mistake, looking bad, or being wrong, so they do research in pursuit of the "perfect" solution or decision. And they won't make a decision until they find it. (And, of course, perfect doesn't usually exist, so they don't buy at all.) That is where you want to be assumptive in a powerful way.

When our mind can't make a decision, it gets confused about what is the correct path to take. When prospects feel confused, their default response will be "No," "I need to think about it," or "Send me more information." A confused mind never buys.

CONSULTATIVE CLOSE

You may have noticed a distinct lack of sales tactics, slick lines, and structured "closes." That was intentional because I think most salespeople are failing to use some fundamental sales-related practices, especially salespeople who operate more like order takers, which is why most of this book was designed to help you build a proper foundation first.

But if you made it this far, patiently building your sales success foundation, then you have arrived at the two foundational closes I feel are universally effective. The first is the consultative close. This strategy is meant to counteract the analysis paralysis trap that plagues order-taking salespeople and their unsuspecting prospects who end up dying a terrible, non-purchasing death in the rep's pipeline. If we look at what makes for a good consultant, the generally accepted ideal process is to start asking questions of the prospective client with the goal of uncovering their pain, issues, goals, and/or desires (like we talked about in Chapter 10). From there, the consultative-minded person puts together a plan with suggestions customized to that individual or their business, with the ultimate goal of helping them get to their more ideal state.

In my experience, salespeople who follow that same sales model are able to produce successful, long-term results. You don't need to have the title *consultant* to act like a consultant. The key is to use questions and discovery to arrive at a diagnosis, like a doctor. Then you make an assumption based on all the data you have received. The assumptive part is centered on what the prospect should do. This type of strategy works because you are assum-

ing they should do *blank* because of your experience as a professional. To avoid analysis paralysis, take on a consultant's role to
narrow their options to one or two of the best solutions. When
the options are limited, the decision becomes easier. Instead of
five packages to choose from, you determine the top solution
for them based on their individual situation. Your doctor would
never give you five prescriptions to choose from, so stop feeling
like you should give your prospects that many. They are looking
to you as the professional. I give you permission to act like one!
Present the smallest number of options; then guide them to pick
one, or narrow it down to one. Then proceed to the next step.

ASSUMPTIVE CLOSE

Now you are ready for the Assumptive Close, which is ridiculously
simple to understand, but not always easy to do: Assume the deal.
What does that mean? You build trust (again: rapport + empathy +
questions + active listening), identify the ideal solution with your
prospect via your consultative close process, and then assume they
want to purchase.

Where most reps get it wrong is in asking for permission. That is
simply not necessary when the process is done correctly. Now, I
need to clarify something before those experienced in sales start
sending me hateful messages—asking for permission to close is different than earning permission to close. You must always earn permission to close, which is based on having built the proper level of
trust with the prospect, being viewed as a professional, and having
enough information to provide the best solution for them. Once you
have met those three criteria, you have earned permission to close.

When you get to that point, the key is not to ask them if they
want to buy. Just assume they do. Always assume the sale and
close—again, only when you have earned permission. If the
prospect doesn't want to buy, or has concerns, they will stop

you. Referring back to the doctor example, your doctor will go through their process, tell you their diagnosis, and give you a prescription. They don't say, "Your arm is broke. Would you like me to set it and put it in a cast?" No, they say, "Your arm is broke. We need to set it and put it in a cast." Then you get some pain meds and schedule a follow-up exam. And if you disagree with their prescription, you can stop them, but they won't usually ask if you would like to "buy" treatment. At most, they will direct you to pick from alternative options. By showing up at the doctor's office, or emergency room, you are giving them permission to help you get to a better condition. When your prospects walk into your store, fill out your web form, call your toll-free number, or even answer your calls and go through your questions, they are giving you some level of permission to help them. First, make sure you earn permission. Then, assume the sale and don't stop unless they stop you.

Why is the assumptive close such a game-changer for most salespeople? Order takers ask for permission. "Would you like to sign up?" "Would you like to buy this one?" "What do you think?" Questions like that leave the decision up to the prospect, who, as we already discussed, is potentially living with some level of fear of change (and mentally reliving an experience where a salesperson took advantage of them). When you ask these types of questions, you open the door to a "need to think about it," "not at this time," or "call me in a month" conversation-killing statement. Order takers ask, but sales superstars gather information and then assume they know what is best.

The main caveat with assumptive selling is to, once again, make sure your intentions are in the right place for your prospects' sake. Salespeople who assume the sale and steamroll prospects into buying regardless of fit have given sales professionals a bad name in most of the world, causing buyer's remorse (see Chapter 18), cancels (see Chapter 17), and complaints. Please use your powers for good and not evil!

ASSUMING EXERCISES

How well do you use a consultative and assumptive type process to get your prospects to purchase?

If you didn't rate yourself a 10, what can you use from this chapter to be consultative and assumptive once you know what the process should do?

_____

_____

_____

_____

_____

_____

_____

_____

_____

_____

_____

_____

_____

SUMMARY

The biggest lesson I (Jason) learned early in my sales career was that asking for permission and giving too many options meant certain death for a large percentage of sales interactions. I discovered the goal of using questions to collect information was to sell in a consultative way by providing customized solutions based on benefiting the prospect, whether they were struggling and needed help, or were wanting to buy something and unsure which one to pick. Luckily, I never prejudged because, by the time I got into sales, I had experienced prejudging as a customer. In fact, there was a period when, to test jewelry salespeople, I would purposefully dress like an average college student to see which salespeople at which stores would acknowledge my presence. The ones eager to help got access to the wad of cash I had with me.

Like with most things, there are ways a skill can be used for positive or negative results. Assuming is no different. When used incorrectly, sales reps will make judgmental decisions with incomplete information that will lead to potentially dismissing or ignoring qualified and interesting prospects. Don't do that.

Then there are the consultative and assumptive closes. These are so fundamentally necessary as a part of your standard routine with each prospect that most other closes become secondary or unnecessary. There are always things you can learn, better statements to make, or processes to follow. But when you gather the right information, build the right rapport, and create a level of trust where the prospect views you as a professional, you have earned the right to close. From there, it is about acting how a doctor would: determining—based on questions, answers, and your experience—the correct diagnosis, and then assuming the prescription provided will cure them.

These are the fundamental building blocks of positive persuasion. When you take everything we covered in Section 1: Being Authentic, combined with these last seven chapters, you can make that transformation from order taker to quota breaker. And we still have one more section of the book to go.

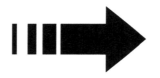

SECTION 3
SALES SUCCESS INTANGIBLES

What are *intangibles*? *Merriam-Webster* defines intangible as "an abstract quality or attribute" or "an asset (such as goodwill) that is not corporeal (material)." In sports, the intangibles are those actions that don't necessarily show up on a stats line, such as "hustle plays" in basketball or "defensive pressure" in football. These small, hard-to-track items can be the difference between winning and losing, especially when playing against other professionals.

Your prospects are highly skilled opponents. The primal parts of the homo sapiens brain have been keeping our species safe for a very long time. No matter how long you have been in your sales career, the survival instincts of the mind have you beat in terms of experience.

The intangibles are required to tip the sales process in your favor if you want to create long-term and consistent sales success. Many salespeople want to skip straight to this section, looking for the perfect tool to achieve instant results. The topics in this section are important but only truly valuable in the hands of someone adding onto the Authentic Persuasion foundation. These intangibles are powerful and effective when layered on top of what we covered in the last two sections.

CHAPTER 14

OBSERVING YOUR OWN OBJECTIONS

"Knowing your own mind is the solution to all our problems."

— Thubten Yeshe

Overall, Gordon was slightly below performance expectations. At best, he hit quota, but more often, he was under quota each week. When Susan, his manager, dove in to identify why Gordon was struggling to convert leads, she found a trend in his notes. Like everyone, he had some prospects who had to talk to their spouses, and some who didn't have time, but a big percentage said they needed to "think about it." This happens to a lot of reps, but the interesting part was that it seemed almost always to happen right after he asked for something major, like their Social Security or credit card number to complete the transaction.

Most people's instinct is to be self-centered. Again, we are human and our default mode is survival. This holds true for salespeople as well. And if you aren't achieving the level of sales success you expect, there is a good chance what is keeping you from closing more deals is that your personal issues and objections are creeping into your conversations. And I would guess you don't even realize it.

In some ways, dealing with prospects is similar to being around animals. Like dogs, prospects can sense fear and insecurity. They can sense weakness and hesitation better than we notice it in ourselves. In this first chapter on the intangibles topic, I am going to discuss fears and doubts relative to how you feel about your product, service, or idea, and how your prospects are telling you everything you need to know about your own issues. Like our own moms, our prospects know us better than we might know ourselves.

SUBCONSCIOUS POWER

In Chapter 3, we talked about how the primal parts of our mind want to keep us safe while operating from our comfort zone. Our mind remembers unpleasant things and it will do what it can to avoid them in the future. We can learn what is safe and what dangers to avoid by going through the pain ourselves. Most people only have to touch a hot stove once to know they don't want to do it again. The alternative is learning from what we see other people go through and deciding to take a different path; however, most people don't navigate life that way.

Throughout life, negative events will happen. Specifically, you, as a customer, sometimes make poor purchasing decisions. We have all done it—bought something on impulse from a really charismatic, smooth-talking salesperson, or given a sales rep all our personal information only to regret it later, or signed up for a service without researching it, only to find out it was not what we expected, wanted, or needed. All of those experiences leave a mark in our minds.

Then you get a sales job. You bring with you either the "hot stoves" you touched as a consumer or stories of other people's regrets. When you are speaking with prospects, working hard to convert them into customers, your subconscious is screaming at you to warn them against feeling the same hurt you felt in the past. The illogical part is that when you know you are one of the "good ones," you shouldn't doubt your product/service or project your issues onto others. Yet, even if it's true that your intentions are good your primal subconscious is still reliving past injuries and projecting those issues and fears onto others.

SILENT (DEAL) KILLER

I have seen salespeople working for companies, drawing a base salary, and showing up each day, with a quota or goal to close deals, who feel negative about some aspects of their product/service/idea. I have also experienced reps who do not agree with how the sales process works. The fascinating part is that most of the time these salespeople do not even realize they have a bias affecting their sales performance.

At the root of that negativity is they don't want to do to others what they don't like others doing to them. For example, if you don't personally believe in making an on-the-spot buying decision (for something of relatively significant cost or value), then that is the filter through which you view the world of sales. You could never imagine walking into a car dealership to just "look around" and walking out a few hours later with a new car. So you create your normal buying process, based on how you operate, plus past impulse buys you've regretted, which would be to research cars, read reviews, check out comparisons online, maybe even go test-drive cars before returning home to think about it. After all that, you might go back and buy one.

People who don't usually buy on the spot yet go into sales find it hard to convince prospects to make on-the-spot decisions to buy because it makes them feel like hypocrites. Even if their prospect is 100 percent qualified for their product or service, and it's a perfect fit to help them achieve their goals, solve their problems, and/or take away their pain, the salesperson would subconsciously default to language that triggers the prospect to say things like: "I'll have to think about it."

Money is another internal, limiting belief that gets in the way of sales success. If you struggle financially, your subconscious will exude scarcity. Or if you are stable financially but couldn't really afford what you are selling, you may not be able to relate to someone buying from you. The vibes you would give off will not instill confidence such that prospects want to move forward.

If you are coming into sales without understanding your internal bias of how you act as a consumer (we all have them) or about money, you will struggle to be successful. And unless you or your manager are very observant, you may not even realize what is causing you to lose deals you could easily close.

HOW IT SHOWS UP

There are two main ways your conscious or subconscious bias shows up in conversations: in how you ask, and how you respond. Let's start with how you are asking for information when you don't believe in it yourself and potentially feel like a hypocrite. Your voice will have a different tone, one that lacks confidence, probably similar to when you were new in your sales role and didn't have confidence in what to say. I have heard reps who sound strong until they get to that one hot button topic in their mind. Then, for some, it's almost like a switch goes off and they sound totally weak and shy, while for others, their discomfort could be very subtle and hard to detect. But it's there.

The issue is that one skill we possess as humans is the ability to make determinations based on what we hear. Again, back to our minds and our comfort zones, most people are constantly on the lookout for danger—real or perceived. Like animals, your prospects can detect fear, and when they ask for information that you personally would not provide or you disagree with asking for, it will come across in your tone. The person you are speaking with will pick up on your hesitation or displeasure, and it will trigger alarm bells in their mind and create objections and issues.

This leads into the second way bias shows up: how you respond. Imagine you just asked your prospect for some private financial information. Your tone was not confident, coming from an internal belief around not wanting to share your own personal information. The prospect detects this and starts to object to handing over the requested data. Because you wouldn't have given out your information if you were on their end, internally, you are agreeing with them. Then, out of your mouth, your response might not be "You're right; I wouldn't give out that info either!", but instead of overcoming their objection, rebuilding trust, and reminding them of why they need or want to buy what you are selling, you let them off the hook. You struggle with putting up a tough persuasive argument if you agree with their position.

I have seen this with sales reps who don't agree with paying fees, being upsold additional products/services, giving out sensitive personal information, providing payment over the phone, buying on the initial call, and signing contracts/agreements. If you are unsure what your biases might be, replay your conversations in your mind and look through the notes on all the deals you didn't close. My experience says you will see some patterns.

STOP PROJECTING

If you are self-aware enough to identify your self-imposed, mental stumbling blocks, congratulations—this is not as common as you might think because most people are living on autopilot. But now that you're aware of this issue, what are your options to overcoming those mindset barriers to create sales success? Start by determining how big of a deal your internal rules are mentally and if there is a way to mitigate those feelings. Is it a barrier coming from deep within your belief system? If you fundamentally disagree with the idea of buying a new car, and think it's a bad financial decision, then don't go into new car sales because you will struggle to generate success. If you don't like giving out personal information over the phone, does that represent a deep core value that is a wall you couldn't ask someone to cross over?

Second, is there a workaround for your internal obstacle? If you would never give out your debit card information without confirming you are dealing with a valid business, what information would you need as a consumer to feel comfortable? Is there a way you would be okay with moving forward? Once you have identified a solution, gather similar information on your organization—websites, brochures, or copies of licenses, etc.—that would help someone who feels like you do be more comfortable providing personal information. This will help you feel in alignment with your core beliefs and mindset. Be sure to have the information on hand when talking with prospects, but be careful you don't trigger their analysis paralysis.

Let me remind you: Doing the right thing for people is always the right thing to do. If you are selling something you believe in *and* you have identified that the other person would truly benefit from it, then it's really important to get your own fears and hesitations out of the way. If you know you are a good person selling a good product/service/idea for the benefit of the other person, then that confidence will help you find solutions to get past any of your internal issues.

OBJECTIONS EXERCISE

Do you have an internal, mental, limiting belief as a buyer that could be affecting your sales performance?

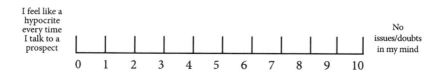

If you didn't rate yourself a 10, what can you use from this chapter to identify where you are bringing your negative thoughts into those discussions?

WHAT IF YOU CAN'T?

The last option, in the event that your mental or emotional barrier is just too strong and you have a constant feeling of dread or feel like a fake, phony, or hypocrite, is to stop trying to sell what you are selling, change companies, or get out of sales. Gary Vaynerchuk says it best, "Life is too short to do shit you hate!" Sometimes you may be tempted to take a job doing something you do not feel good about just to make money. I contend that it's not worth it. Life is truly too short, so do the things you want to do, especially if they use your natural talents and abilities. On the flip side, life is long and painful when you are doing something that goes against your core beliefs.

SUMMARY

Susan was able to identify the subtle signs that Gordon had a mental bias against giving out personal, sensitive information. She found out he had been the victim of identity fraud, and it took him over a year to recover from it. He never wanted that to happen to anyone else, which is why Gordon actually felt bad each time he had to ask for personal information, despite knowing his intentions were good. With some coaching (more like sales therapy), his manager was able to help him identify this internal issue and then provide resources he could use if someone needed help trusting his company. She then kept a close watch to ensure his fears didn't trigger people into research mode, which could cause lost deals.

No matter what we are selling at any given time, the one constant is "you." We are always the ones involved in each thing we do, which means we are bringing the best and worst of ourselves everywhere we go. If we have issues with what we are selling, we will see that reflected in our prospects. Sometimes it will be very obvious, and other times it will be very subtle, through subconscious cues.

It is up to us to recognize our issues and find a way to overcome them or realize they are deal-breakers we cannot resolve and move on to do something else. You will not find long-term success being a hypocrite, asking others to do what you will not do yourself. Imagine if you were afraid of heights and hated the thought of bungee-jumping off a bridge, but due to needing a job, you got hired to be on that bridge helping people get strapped in before jumping. You would think they were crazy, and that would come through in how you interacted with them. You would probably not inspire confidence, especially if they asked you about your bungee-jumping experience and your response was "I would never do that!"

If you determine you can overcome your limiting beliefs, and you are willing to help your prospects move past theirs, then let's keep going. In the next chapter, we will cover the next vital intangible that separates order takers from quota breakers—pausing.

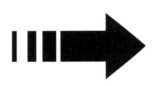

CHAPTER 15

STOP STOPPING

"If you spend too much time thinking about a thing, you'll never get it done."

— Bruce Lee

Carol found herself in sales. She didn't really know how she ended up there; she was just at a junction of desperately needing a job and not knowing what to do with her life. Now she sat at her desk, anxiously thinking about her next call, playing out a stressful scenario in her mind. She had the sales process down and knew what to ask. Where she lost so many opportunities was when prospects started asking her questions. If she had to be on the defensive end of objections or issues, things would fall apart in the conversation. She didn't know what she was missing and started to wonder if she was really meant for sales.

By now, you understand the power of asking questions to uncover your prospects' real motivation. My hope is that you are embracing your duty as a sales professional to help bring your prospects to a better place, whether it means solving a problem or helping them achieve a goal, via your product/service or through a recommendation of what they could do instead.

In Chapter 10, I mentioned that the person asking questions is in control. In this chapter, I will cover one of the hallmark indicators of an order taker—how they handle prospects who are wrestling for control, asking questions, and raising objections.

DEATH BY A THOUSAND PUNCHES

Picture this scenario: You are going through your sales process, maybe even giving the prospect your smooth, well-scripted, natural-sounding monologue about how your product/service works, and then they stop you with a question. Whether their inquiry is simple or an objection, if they throw you a question, it has to be answered. The good news in this scenario is you know the answer, so you provide the ideal and succinct response (unlike dancing, covered in Chapter 9). You are feeling confident about yourself at this point.

After answering, you pause a moment to let your wonderful answer sink in, hopefully, satisfying the prospect and putting their mind at ease. Before moving forward, you want to make sure nothing else is occupying their thoughts, so you pause for a moment more, creating a space where they could address any other concerns. You don't really want to be asked more questions, but you pause anyway. You don't even realize you are doing it.

In this conversational gap, they raise another issue. That's fine because you have more answers. You might worry a little that they could ask something you can't answer, but you could always go find what they need. When they continue to ask questions, it means they have more concerns or there are stumbling blocks in their mind, so the only polite thing to do is allow them the chance to ask, right? And once they are out of questions, you are clear to push for the sale, right?

Before you know it, they have asked you question after question after question. When you have a chance to take a breath, you start to feel like a boxer being punched over and over again, on the ropes, trying to defend yourself, hoping the bell will ring and end the round. Depending on their fear level, combined with their desire to get clarification, and based on your sales and persuasion skills, they may knock you down. Too many questions could lead in one direction—the prospect walking away. You lose the deal; you're knocked out. Death by a thousand punches. In my experience, you won't even realize why they walked, thinking it was because they needed to think about it, feeling like at least you did your part in addressing all their concerns.

WHY PAUSING IS SO BAD

Of course, I want you to be courteous and give people a chance to talk. Please don't think I support salespeople who steamroll prospects, avoid their questions, or dismiss their objections in some kind of manipulative, controlling mind game. All kinds of training programs and books will teach you how to ignore or side-step questions. But if they have concerns burning in their minds, it is best to let them ask. Until they ask, they aren't really going to listen to anything else you are saying anyway.

What is so wrong with answering a question and then giving the person a chance to ask more? Because it hurts your sales success in two ways. First, it goes back to the concept that the person asking the questions is in control. When they ask and you answer, they have taken control. Answering, then pausing, allows them to stay in control. For skilled and experienced salespeople, this is not an issue because they can get control back any time they want. But for most struggling salespeople and order takers, it will generally lead to the death of their sales careers. It all comes down to how many punches (questions/objections/issues) you can take and remain standing.

The second reason pausing is so bad for your sales success has to do with fear, which I covered in Chapter 8. The animal part of our brain fears change and wants to stay in its comfort zone. Buying your product/service represents a change, so the prospect must decide if it's worth the risk. We know sometimes prospects ask questions out of a fear of change. Each will have a certain level of fear or hesitation, and most of the time, it reflects their comfort zone and personal rules on making decisions. If you allow them to ask question after question after question without taking back control of the process and leading them back to why they want what you are offering in the first place, they will ultimately convince themselves it is safer not to buy. Your goal is not to let them stay put; your goal is to help them make the right buying decision. Allowing them to stay in control will allow them to prove to themselves it's better to stay in their comfort zone. At that moment, you have lost.

WHY PAUSING HAPPENS

Before we can talk about what to do instead of having pause-filled conversations, it is important to understand why it happens. Until you know the why, you can't change the what. I already alluded to it, but pausing happens, typically, as a result of the people-pleasing part of our brains. Of course, everyone is different, and this is more of a priority for some than others.

If you lean toward people-pleasing, you want the other person to be happy and feel satisfied. If people-pleasing is your dominant trait and you are in a sales position, your default operating mode will be to ensure the prospect is satisfied in every way with your product/service, process, and even you as the salesperson before they decide to buy. The small, and typically unnoticed, act of pausing after answering a question is your subconscious way of ensuring space for the prospect to ask additional questions or raise more issues or objections. Part of you is encouraging them to ask all their questions to ensure they are 100 percent ready to buy. Even if you have some level of fear about overcoming their concerns, you don't want any issues to go unvoiced.

There is also an aspect of asking questions and controlling the conversation that could trigger confrontation with the prospect. Somewhere in our brain are memories of questions that led to arguments. Now in your sales role, you think that asking too many questions, controlling the conversation, or moving forward without ensuring the prospect is totally on board will cause drama. Maybe you have even had a prospect snap at you or get confrontational. Maybe they even said things like, "You are just trying to get me to buy so you can make a commission," or "I am not going to buy right now no matter how much you try to pressure me." Those scenarios are still in your subconscious, and if you are not careful, they will restrict your actions from fear they might happen again.

A third cause of pausing instead of regaining control is that maybe you have negative experiences of controlling-type behavior. You may have grown up with a controlling family member or been in a relationship with a controlling person. Consequently, you don't like feeling controlled, which is why you stay away from anything even close to controlling behavior. So, as you sit there in front of a prospect, your mind keeps you from taking certain actions.

DON'T PAUSE

I want to reiterate that nothing is inherently wrong with pausing and ensuring your prospect is satisfied before making their decision. Being a "people-pleaser" is not negative, and it definitely has its place. The challenge is knowing when and if it can be effective in closing deals, not just taking orders.

Unless you are in customer service, you need to break yourself of the habit of inserting potentially damaging pauses after your responses. The solution is fundamentally simple but not always easy: Don't pause. Pausing has killed more sales than I could possibly have counted in my years of managing salespeople. Stop pausing after you respond if you want to win at the game of sales and have long-term success.

As to my customer service comment, I think pausing to ensure your customer is satisfied is a valuable skill in customer service. That people-pleasing trait is vital when the goal is to ensure customer satisfaction, especially if the interaction was triggered by a problem, issue, question, or need. I would challenge you, if you lean more toward the people-pleasing, order taker end of the spectrum, to look deep into yourself and consider the possibility that a customer service or account manager role is actually the place for you and would lead to more personal and professional success.

WHAT TO DO INSTEAD: RETURN TO QUESTION

Based on your desire to improve your selling skills, then let's talk about what to do in place of pausing. Since we know pausing is ineffective, the first option is to address your prospect's concern in a satisfactory way, and then pick up where you left off.

I call it "Return to Question" because most of the time, objections come up in response to a question you ask the prospect. Sometimes they come up during your monologue, but generally, its when you are pushing the prospect for information, which triggers their fear of change or lack of trust. Your questions are like poking a stick at their comfort zone bubble. That is when they will get a little defensive (or sometimes really, really defensive) avoid answering, and ask you a question back.

Here is an example of what the interaction and pause looks like:

You: Would you like to put this on a debit card or credit card?

Prospect: [Realizing this transaction is getting real.] Can I cancel if I am not happy with it?

You: Yes, you can cancel at any time. [Answer provided, talking stopped, pause initiated.]

Prospect: What are my options for canceling?

You: If you want to cancel, you can either call our customer service team or make the request in writing. Just make sure you do it five days before your billing date or the payment will go through anyway, and you will then need to wait for a refund. [Answered. Stopped. Paused.]

Prospect: Do you have a way I can try it out before signing up?

You: [continue to answer questions; keep pausing after each one.]

Prospect: [continues to ask questions]

Remember, the person asking questions is in control. When the prospect hits you with an objection or issue, they are grasping for control. They are trying to determine whether it's safe to proceed. Your strategy is to address their question, concern, or need for information, and then return to the question you had asked.

Here is what a more effective way looks like:

You: Would you like to put this on a debit card or credit card?

Prospect: [Realizing this transaction is getting real.] Can I cancel if I am not happy with it?

You: Yes, you can cancel at any time. Did you want to use a debit or credit card?

Most reps would have answered the question and then paused. Instead, you can see that you don't want to pause. You want to Return to Question. You were asking a question; they ignored it and asked their question. Answer their question, return to your question, and don't pause.

WHAT TO DO INSTEAD: EMPATHETIC REVERSING

Traditional sales training might tell you to use a tactic called "reversing," which is the act of answering a question with a question. In the above example, you might have been trained to say, "Why would you want to cancel?" Sometimes this will work, but if you use reversing (not answering their questions but just asking a new question instead) every time, it will annoy the prospect—and it usually comes across as confrontational or passive-aggressive. Rarely does using reversing as the main objection-handling tactic produce long-term sales success. Usually, it just triggers the prospect to put up bigger walls and retreat further into the safety of their comfort zone.

However, I have used a modified form of reversing for years and found it very effective in certain situations. I call it "Empathetic Reversing." It is a deeper-level approach to take when met with a question or concern. Let's look at how to use it by revisiting our previous example, picking up where we left off:

You: Yes, you can cancel at any time. Did you want to use a debit or credit card?

Prospect: So, what is the process for canceling if I am unhappy?

(Notice that the prospect still isn't answering the question—a huge red flag that what they are asking about is a hot button issue for them.)

You: If you want to cancel, you can either write to us or call our customer service team. Just make sure you do it five days before your billing date or the payment will go through anyway, and you will need to wait for a refund. *Let me ask you, why are you concerned about canceling?*

Prospect: I signed up with a program like this last year, and they didn't do what they said they would. Then, when I went to cancel, it was a pain in the butt. I want to make sure that if this doesn't work, I can get out of it easily.

A lot actually occurred in this short back and forth so let's dissect it. First, notice that the prospect didn't answer the question a second time. Again, that is a sign the issue is important to them. Often, people ask questions out of curiosity or to check a box mentally. Then, at the other end of the spectrum are the burning concerns that could be deal-breakers if the prospect doesn't trust you, your company, or the product/service. Asking a second time about the same issue should prompt you to shift from using Return to Question to Empathetic Reversing.

Next, notice that the response became about addressing the concern a second, deeper time, but with a twist. You can see that the second response ended with, "Let me ask you, why are you concerned about canceling?" This is the Empathetic Reversing part because it's not just about answering a question with a question—you give them an answer but then ask why it's important to them. The key difference is that you actually care (the *empathy* part) about why they are concerned. You want to know the deeper reason, instead of just throwing back the response you were trained to use.

The other vital key is in *how* you say the last part, which is why I call it Empathetic Reversing. Many salespeople will ask in a defensive, combative way. When they do that, they might win the mental/emotional battle, but they will always lose the war (sale). Instead, you need to speak from a place of actually caring about the other person. (For fun, practice the above dialogue in your mind, first in a caring way, then in a defensive "salesy" way to hear how well it can and cannot work.)

The end result of Empathetic Reversing should be you learning something you wouldn't have found out if you hadn't asked the second part. That piece of information is what you are after. It will allow you to address their real fear, usually based on something negative that happened to them, or someone they know. If you can help them feel comfortable with your solution, provide evidence that they can trust your company, or ensure they fully understand their options, you will have a much more solid deal. And if you use Return to Question and Empathetic Reversing, you will have almost fully graduated from order taker to quota breaker!

PAUSING EXERCISE

It can be hard to assess without listening to your sales interactions, but how well do you move through the conversation without pausing?

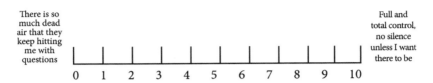

There is so
much dead
air that they
keep hitting
me with
questions

Full and
total control,
no silence
unless I want
there to be

0   1   2   3   4   5   6   7   8   9   10

If you didn't rate yourself a 10, what can you use from this chapter to cut down on the damaging silence?

_____

_____

_____

_____

_____

_____

_____

_____

_____

_____

SUMMARY

Carol's issue was that she prided herself on being a salesperson who ensured her prospects felt pleased. Really, that is not the issue, and truthfully, the world could use more salespeople like Carol. The challenge was at the intersection of kindness (Carol) and sales. Carol realized she could help more people by effectively moving them forward to buy from her. She knew if qualified prospects didn't buy from her, they would find someone else who likely wouldn't care about them as much as she did. Carol learned it was possible for her to care about her customers, address their concerns, stay in control, *and* close deals.

One of the hallmark traits of an order taker is the habit of pausing after answering a question, whether it's a full-blown objection or just curiosity. Order takers tend to act like people pleasers, and they generalize that to be a successful salesperson takes being an uncaring, commission seeker who goes for the jugular by being pushy and/or controlling. That couldn't be any further from the truth. A successful salesperson who is in it for the long term is focused on maintaining positive control of the sales process, closing well above quota, and ensuring their prospects are satisfied with the purchase.

The issue with pausing is that it creates a vacuum, and in that vacuum, the prospect's mind retreats into their cozy comfort zone, and they will continue to hit you with more questions. Your best tools for a successful sales career are: Return to Question and Empathetic Reversing. Both, when used properly, will elevate your conversation and lead to more deals. Your job is to be a professional, like the doctor we discussed previously. When you do that, you are in control, and your intention is actually getting the prospect to a better place as a result of working with you. As Dale Carnegie says, "When dealing with people, remember you are not dealing with creatures of logic."

To become an Authentic Persuader takes controlling the conversation and eliminating the pauses. In the next chapter, we will cover the next sales success intangible: what happens if you don't close the deal and have to follow up.

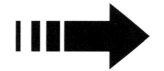

CHAPTER 16

AVOIDING THE FOLLOW-UP TRAP

*"Every sale has five obstacles: no need, no money,
no hurry, no desire, no trust."*

— Zig Ziglar

They had a routine that went like clockwork each day. It felt normal and natural, and when it was done, Bob would get busy. He would sit in the office, with his yellow pad, while his manager pulled all of Bob's leads in the system to go through the status of each one that had yet to close. One by one, Bob would share an excited comment about how they were going to call him back by the end of the week to sign up, or that he was calling them on such-and-such a date to follow up, or that they needed to talk to so-and-so, and once they did that, they would be ready to buy. This pipeline review process happened day in and day out. Bob had "so many good leads that were right on the edge of closing," he proclaimed. Yet the reality was, no matter how great his pipeline was, Bob's performance was constantly at the bottom of his peers, and most months, he struggled to make quota, let alone earn commissions.

In any sales role, ideally, you want to ask your questions, uncover your prospects' greatest needs, and close them during the first interaction—one and done! In some industries, that is the only option for their sales model. If that is you, where there is an expectation of 100 percent one-call closes, with no follow-ups, then this chapter isn't for you. This is for everyone selling something that has some ratio of on-the-spot purchases and follow-up conversations to move the prospect forward to the close. (Note: If you have a long sales cycle where no one buys on the first call, this chapter could also help you.)

The most accurate indicator I have found for identifying order takers is the effectiveness of their follow-up calls to unclosed leads. There is nothing wrong with having a pipeline of leads to call back and move forward. The issue is whether those leads: a) answer when you call (especially if you had an appointment set), b) have taken needed actions on their end and want to move forward, or c) call you when they say they will. If you cannot answer the question, "Why do they need to buy from us?" (for their reasons, not yours), then you didn't go deep enough in your process with the prospect. If you don't know why they should buy from you—what problem you can solve, pain you can take away, goal you can help them achieve, or desire you fulfill—then how can you expect them to know it well enough to buy? This chapter will help improve the results of your pipeline, but it will usually take a challenging shift for those of you behaving like order takers.

THE RIGHT RATIO OF ONE-CALL CLOSING

Before we can get to the cause and solution of the follow-up trap, we must examine the one-call close. Now, I use the term "one call" to mean any time your prospect buys during the first interaction with you. While this might seem like it's just about phone sales, this concept also applies to in-person sales as well (and whatever industry you are in, you probably have your own term for this first-interaction-sale).

Every business I have seen with a consultative sales process has an ideal ratio of one-call closes per rep. While it might seem like the obvious ratio is 100 percent, that is not generally true. If you have a consultative sales approach with a product or service that requires some effort on the buyer's behalf, then it will never, and should never, be 100 percent.

"Why wouldn't my goal be 100 percent?" you might ask. There are times when a buyer might not qualify "right now" but could take some steps to get there (maybe fixing their credit, or securing more money, or getting another party involved—cosigner, spouse, boss), or you need items or information from them that they do not have available (like their bank routing/account numbers, vital documents, or other parties who need to sign). No matter how hard you want to push for the sale in the moment, there are prospects who just aren't ready.

Before you start writing a nasty email to me, yes, I know that it's never about the money; it's about the value, and if there is enough value, someone will find the money. And yet, there are still times when people see the value and need to take steps to get the money to complete the transaction (which then changes it from a one-call close to a follow-up deal).

FOR EVERYTHING ELSE THERE ARE FOLLOW-UPS

Because of the above factors, professional sales organizations will not have a 100 percent one-call close ratio. If they did, it would mean they were leaving money on the table by losing all the prospects who had to go off and do something before moving the process forward. When a rep has a 100 percent one-call-close ratio, it means they are pushing people to buy now and ignoring anyone who doesn't, can't, or won't. An example would be a door-to-door sales crew that visits a neighborhood, knocks on doors, makes sales, then moves on to the next location never to speak with those people who weren't ready to buy that day.

At the other end of the spectrum, when a rep has a very low one-call-close ratio, it means their one-call-close deals were eager prospects ("laydowns") and the majority of their deals rely on callbacks. Classic metrics of an order taker.

If you don't close all your deals in one call, then you have follow-ups, whether you call them or they call you. Again, my point is that I am not anti-follow-ups. In fact, the previous section explains why I feel follow-ups are necessary to any professional salesperson's process.

WHY THEY DON'T ANSWER/RESPOND

Having a pipeline of follow-up leads is an important component of a professional salesperson's success because it will provide that extra sales volume to help earn bigger commissions. But if you have ever had a pipeline full of leads that haven't bought from you yet, then you know the frustration you feel when they don't answer for the set call back appointments or the unscheduled follow-ups, and they aren't calling you back either. They just seem to have moved on or put their head back in the sand.

Why does this happen? Here is the brutal truth—most likely, you failed as a sales professional. If they were qualified candidates, and you didn't close them at the moment, and the majority of them have now gone into what I call the "prospect witness protection program," then you blew it. I know that probably stings the ego a little, and you might be feeling defensive and want to argue that it's not your fault. But it is, and the sooner you realize it and take responsibility, the sooner we can get you from order taker to quota breaker!

How can I make that statement and think it applies to everyone who reads this book? Because your sales process should start by asking questions and verifying qualifications. Once you have determined if someone qualifies, you also must determine what problem they are trying to solve or which goal they want to achieve. Your questions, as we covered, should be used to dive as deeply as possible—the deeper the better. Once you know the *why* you can solve, your only job becomes helping them see the value of your product/service. If they cannot buy right now, need a follow-up, and dodge your calls, it means you didn't get them to see the value of your solution for *their* reasons. Not your self-centered salesperson reasons, but what it meant to them and why.

Now, to let you off the hook a little, I acknowledge there are times when the prospect's situation changes, and there is nothing you can do about it. I have seen situations where between the initial call and the follow-up, someone has passed away, filed for bankruptcy, lost a job, changed jobs, or been diagnosed with a terminal illness. This is referred to as "life," and there is nothing you can do about it. I could argue that if you had closed them in one call, it would have got you the sale before any of those situations came up; therefore, you still ultimately lost the sale. However, and this is critical if your prospect gets hit hard by *life*, I am never upset that I "didn't close them sooner," and I am not unhappy if they bought, and then something happened and they called to cancel. I have been through enough *life* to know there is nothing you can do about it. Never beat yourself up and say, "If only I had pushed them to close, I would have got the deal." Forcing deals in a race against the *life* of your prospect will only lead to cancellations, returns, or unhappy clients.

WHAT SHOULD YOU DO WITH YOUR PIPELINE?

If the majority of your pipeline is unresponsive when you reach out to them, you have fallen into the Follow-up Trap. I am not referring to leads who need to be nurtured. I am talking about the obviously qualified leads who end up ghosting you. Most reps

I meet have already fallen into this dark hole of deals that will likely never resurface, and most of the time, little can be done to revive them.

If you realize you are already deep into the Follow-up Trap where your pipeline is in this unresponsive mode, it means the expectations with the prospects were set poorly in the first place, and I hate being the one to tell you this, but they are pretty much garbage.

First, don't give up on your current pipeline. Continue to follow up with the proper cadence, and hopefully, some prospects will convert. There is always a chance that the timing will be right, independent of your initial conversation and efforts. Second, make sure to set the proper expectations in your mind and with your manager. Stop telling your manager about all the great leads you have and how you should hear from them soon and get them closed. Stop thinking and hoping that your pipeline will help you make quota, and definitely stop banking on it to earn a bonus. If it happens, it is luck.

Ultimately, you may need to give your pipeline to another rep, where a fresh voice leaving messages or sending emails could make the difference in turning prospects into deals. At this point, those prospects are done, unless they realize why they should buy from you on their own. And the more you call them, chasing after what should have been a deal, the deeper their heads will go into the sand.

HOW TO AVOID THE FOLLOW-UP TRAP

Now that we have the harsh reality out of the way, the second and more vital step is to change what you are doing in your conversations this very moment and moving forward. The best solution is prevention. The key is to stop planting rotten seeds in the ground, and instead, plant seeds that have the potential to yield a harvest. If you put even half of what we have covered in this book so far into action, you will find that you quickly have prospects answering when you call back, replying to email, or showing up for appointments.

When you ask questions with the intention of digging deeply enough to find out why the prospect needs (not just wants) to buy your product or service, then you are moving in the right direction. Your goal should be to determine if they are a qualified buyer for your company; at that point, it shouldn't be a matter of if they need to buy from you. Since there are times when they won't buy during the initial meeting and a follow-up is warranted, you will still have a pipeline full of follow-ups.

Please understand that the issue is not the follow-up; the issue is the setup to the follow-up. Let me give you an example. Imagine you are feeling pain in your side. It has become so constant and unbearable that you decide to go to the doctor. She examines you to the best of her abilities in the office but cannot determine what the cause is. The doctor sends you to the lab to get your blood drawn. You're told to expect a call from her office around three the next afternoon with news.

If you have ever been in this situation, you know how it will go. That night, you probably won't sleep very well, not just from the pain but also from the worry and stress of waiting and what-ifing yourself to sleep. The next morning, you look at your work schedule to make sure you are available around three o'clock that afternoon. Starting at around one, you check your phone constantly to ensure the volume is up or it's at least on vibrate so you will know when the doctor calls. As three approaches, you aren't getting anything done; instead, you are constantly checking your phone and thinking of what the doctor might tell you.

Then, your phone rings at 3:04, and you answer it after one ring, even though someone is in your office talking with you. If it had been your boss, you still would have found a way to answer it. The doctor gives you the diagnosis, tells you about the cause and the treatment, and you sit back in your chair relieved to have a diagnosis and a plan.

Has this ever happened to you? Maybe it was with a doctor's diagnosis. Maybe it was a call you were hoping to get about a job you interviewed for. Maybe it was an update about the place you were trying to rent or the house you wanted to buy. We have all gone through that anxious scenario where time stands still, where you shift the world around you to ensure you are available for that important call.

Don't get me wrong—pretty much none of the people reading this book are purveyors of life-or-death information or solutions. You are most likely not a brain or heart surgeon. At the end of the pay period or quarter or year, it might feel like "life or death," but if you are being honest, you know it's not. And no matter how vital your solution is to your customers, most of the time, it's not life or death for them either.

That said, if you are three minutes late calling your prospects for a scheduled appointment or show up a few minutes late to a meeting (which I never advocate...always be on time!), you want them thinking, "Oh, no, maybe that means they aren't going to help me!" That is the level you want to strive for. When you achieve the skills to inspire that feeling of urgency in your conversations, then your pipeline is an amazing thing, full of value and commissions.

Use your questions to uncover your prospect's pain or goals, and then press hard on how you can help them achieve a better state. When done correctly, they should be anticipating your call and actually looking forward to it. When you are a sales professional, your solution will change their life in some way, and they should place anticipating your call toward the waiting for the doctor to call end of the spectrum—not adding your number to their phone under caller ID as "Do Not Answer."

FOLLOW-UP EXERCISE

How well do you know why each person in your pipeline needs what you are selling?

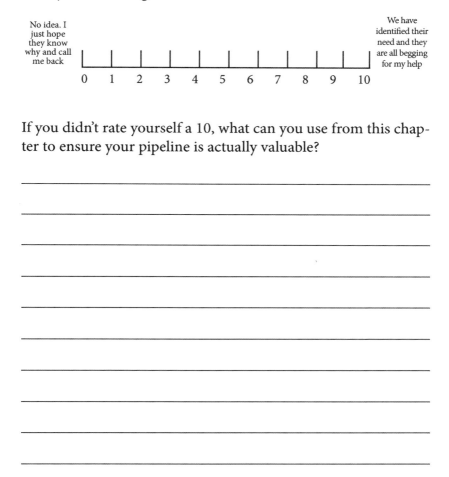

No idea. I just hope they know why and call me back

0 1 2 3 4 5 6 7 8 9 10

We have identified their need and they are all begging for my help

If you didn't rate yourself a 10, what can you use from this chapter to ensure your pipeline is actually valuable?

_____

_____

_____

_____

_____

_____

_____

_____

_____

_____

_____

SUMMARY

It was early Monday morning before most of the team arrived. Bob was there early to speak with his manager. He had realized the truth about his pipeline—that it was not going to yield the deals he proclaimed each day. And it was time for him to stop selling his boss, and start selling his prospects. Bob could see, replaying conversations in his mind, that he wasn't doing his part correctly upfront, which was causing his prospects to be unresponsive later. If his manager had asked him the vital question for each of his pipeline prospects, "Why do you want or need to buy from us?" he would not have had an answer for even a single one of them. This was now going to change as Bob committed to following a more effective sales process.

If you seem to have a low show rate of scheduled appointments, answer rate on follow-up calls or email, and pretty much no proactive contacts by the prospects in your pipeline, then you have fallen deeply into the Follow-Up Trap. The prospects who were clear about how your product/service benefitted them bought during the first interaction. If they didn't buy in one call/visit, and you don't know why they should have, you lost. Your prospect's lack of response is indicating you didn't go deep enough with them.

The solution is easy: Do most of what we have covered in the book so far. When you shift from order taker to sales professional, you will build trust, use questions like a doctor, and then clearly diagnose your prospects. Then, if the deal isn't completed right away and requires a follow-up, you and the prospect both know why they should be excited for your callback. You are on your way to being a quota breaker.

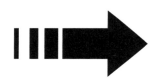

CHAPTER 17

ADDRESSING THE CANCELLATION PARADOX

"You can't make an omelet without breaking eggs."

— Unknown

Karen was proudest of her sales performance stat: zero cancellations in the last three months. Her customers had the ability to cancel after signing up, and of course, the company had a retention and customer service team that worked to save deals and keep customers happy. But Karen never had any cancellations and rarely had anyone even try. She felt good about it because, in her mind, that meant she only enrolled people who were happy with her company and truly wanted its service. She was especially pleased since most of her coworkers had many cancellations during the same period. Yet, her manager was unhappy with her performance. Yes, her cancellations were at zero, but her closing percentage and sales volume were also low.

No one wants customers to cancel a service or return an item. That usually signals the salesperson didn't do well with the customer, which is bad for business, right? Well, that is what most order takers think. But in my experience, a good salesperson has some level of cancellations/returns. When they have none, it is a red flag. Show me a sales rep with zero cancellations, and I guarantee they also have a low closing percentage.

Please understand I am not advocating a lot of cancellations. High percentages indicate a salesperson is not doing things properly on the other end of the spectrum. That type of rep is dangerous to the organization from a financial and reputation management standpoint. But the order taking rep with zero cancellations and a low-closing percentage is also a hazard to the organization's bottom line. In this chapter, I will share why that is and argue the logic for where you want to be.

THE CANCELLATION PARADOX

A paradox is defined as two seemingly absurd or contradictory statements that, when you dive deeper, are valid. The Cancellation Paradox states that a true professional will have an acceptable number of cancellations/returns that is greater than zero. Furthermore, as I stated above, if you have zero cancellations/returns, you are not operating as a salesperson. The Cancellation Paradox holds true for nearly every product or service.

The paradox is that most would not think cancellations or returns would be acceptable. When I explain this principle to sales reps, managers, and owners, at first, they all look at me like I have two heads, both of which are being ridiculous. They don't believe a rep needs some number of unhappy buyers before they can truly be operating like a salesperson.

The even more challenging part to understand is how this fits into the whole discussion of going from order taker to quota breaker. Up to this point, I have been talking about what it means to be a sales professional and how you want to solve the prospect's problems using questions and persuasion, not manipulation and tricks. That I would now suggest—no, promote—the idea of a certain level of unhappy buyers as the litmus test of a true sales superstar seems counterintuitive. But it's not. Please, read the rest of this chapter before giving up on me.

DEFINITION OF A CANCELLATION

First, I feel like I need to address what a cancellation is as I am using it here. If you are signing consumers up for a service, a cancellation means they want to discontinue your service shortly after it starts—as opposed to those who cancel two years later. Again, this could apply to telephone or in-person sales. For example, imagine you are a salesperson at a gym, you sign up someone, and then they decide to cancel a month later.

Some services have zero ability for the customer to cancel or "return" what they bought. A mortgage or home would be an example. Someone isn't going to take out a mortgage to buy a home and then decide they don't like it and try to return it a month later. If unhappy, they are stuck with that decision. However, a stage in the process usually requires trust and transfer of significant information (Social Security number, tax returns, etc.), which requires some level of sales and precision ability to complete. When a prospect cancels their application after this step, I treat that similarly to the previous example. A "sale" took place in accomplishing that major milestone that required all that info, yet the rest of the transaction failed to occur. Some might say this is just a dead lead from the pipeline, but I would put it under the category I am discussing here.

WHAT ZERO CANCELLATIONS MEANS

All right, let's talk about what zero cancellations means and why it is such a bad sign. When you have a cancellation/return rate of zero, it means all your customers are happy with what they purchased. Maybe it's because they liked you, trusted you, you did an amazing job, they felt like you cared about them, you and they became friends during your time together, and then they bought from you. What you sold them is exactly what they wanted, at a price they were happy with, and they would never imagine returning it or calling to cancel. Any or all of those could be true.

If you have made it this far in the book, or you have listened to my podcast, or read anything else I have published, the scenario described above seems to be exactly what I want all sales professionals to aim for, right? Yes…and no.

Yes, those are my ideal sales interactions with every prospect. But no, that is not the only option. When you have zero cancellations, it means you are operating like an order taker. Now, there is a chance you are so amazing that you have both a high closing percentage and zero cancellations, but that will almost never be the case, and later in this chapter, I will explain why.

When you are an order taker in a sales role, you're mainly selling to those people who are ready and do not need much help deciding. There is usually no persuading going on. As we saw in Chapter 8, a purchasing decision involves some level of fear about change. If the prospect has no fear you must overcome, then what you have is a simple transaction—the type of deal that could be done online and wouldn't need a salesperson, maybe could have been processed by a customer service rep. For these *laydowns*, a salesperson is not actually needed. Order takers can handle those well enough.

The issue is, if you are in sales, and your company has a sales department, an actual need exists to sell the product/service, so if you are only closing the easy sales—selling to people ready to buy—you aren't using persuasion. To go from order taker to quota breaker requires pushing some prospects out of their comfort zones and showing them why they should buy from you. That will move you into a higher closing bracket but also trigger some cancellations.

WHAT ABOUT A LOT OF CANCELLATIONS?

I'm not saying lots of cancellations are a good thing. I'm saying a certain number of cancellations indicates a salesperson is making sales, not just taking orders, and excessive cancellations mean a salesperson is not acting with the buyers' best interests in mind. What is excessive? That is specific to your industry and business model—for some, 10 percent could be terrible, for others, it could be 25 percent, or maybe even 5 percent.

How does one rack up cancellations? Poor expectation setting, misleading sales tactics, and inappropriate intentions. Cancellations come from salespeople using manipulation to make money, usually from the wrong prospects, those who shouldn't be buying or signing up in the first place. Essentially, these salespeople are doing all they can to get everyone to buy from them, even the wrong people, which typically leads to lots of cancellations.

This type of salesperson is ultimately dangerous to the business. These cancellations usually lead to a higher percentage of complaints, which, in this era, will most likely end up online for everyone to see. When a company or its sales team is using manipulation and classic "salesy" tactics to generate revenue, it will also have a reputation problem.

THE RIGHT BALANCE OF CANCELLATIONS

If zero cancellations is bad and lots are worse, then what is the right balance? I am not trying to avoid providing a number, but like most topics in this book, the answer is that it depends and will be specific to your industry or company. But there is certainly an acceptable number of cancellations, and this balanced number indicates you are a sales professional and not just an order taker.

When you have the right number of cancellations relative to your sales, it means you are using persuasion to push people forward. The fundamental requirement is that you have done your prequalification step and determined the prospect is a good fit for your product/service, and what you have to offer will help them achieve a goal, be happy, or solve a problem. Once you determine that, you are now in sales mode.

As a salesperson, you are going to encounter prospects who are very afraid of change, yet are qualified customers. You know they need or want your service/product, and intellectually, they do too. But they could still resist or come up with excuses out of fear. This can be especially painful when it's obvious to you as a salesperson that what you are providing will really help them get to a better place. If you want to close those sales, it will take a bit more pushing and pulling, going a bit harder to the close. A sales professional will overcome objections and obstacles, not letting the prospect stop the process with excuses. They will make the prospect a bit uncomfortable (triggering self-preservation, primal brain comfort zone mode), and this will lead to have a higher closing percentage, which could lead to cancellations.

KNOWING WHERE THEY COME FROM

When I was selling, I was aware of when I was pushing prospects a little harder to take action on what they needed. Again, keep in mind that I only did it when they qualified, and I knew I was, ultimately, helping them with our service. I wasn't selling crap to people who didn't need it, and I wasn't lying to people about what our company did for them just to close deals. I have always had a high closing percentage *and* a certain number of cancellations.

The key is I always knew where the cancellations would come from. When I came in and had a voicemail or email from a client I had signed up recently, I was not surprised at all. How did I know they might cancel? Because I had persuaded them to take a leap outside of their comfort zone by making some kind of change. I got them to trust me enough to take that leap. And yet, I knew afterwards it would be that purchase decision versus eons of evolutionary conditioning in their mind. I am a really skilled persuader, but at times, I know I might not win that battle.

There will always be certain scenarios that could lead to a cancellation or return. One example was when I was talking to someone who wanted to check with another party, like their spouse, parent, uncle, friend, etc. It wasn't about me not wanting them to talk to someone else before buying. In fact, I would do all I could to get that other person involved right away. But if that wasn't an option, I would do my best to move the transaction forward anyway, without waiting.

I knew they needed what I was selling, and I wasn't going to let things wait, because experience has taught me that even if you do everything correctly to avoid the Follow-Up Trap, if they didn't buy then, they would put their head back in the sand. So I used Authentic Persuasion to move those types of deals forward, even though they held the greatest chance of cancellations, with a phone call coming later on, maybe from an upset spouse or parent. If they canceled, I knew I had done the right thing because they did, in fact, need what I was offering, even if the other person didn't understand and was trying to "protect" the prospect (i.e., their own fears projected onto my client to keep them safely in their comfort zone).

CANCELLATION EXERCISE

How would you rate your closing percentage and cancel/return percentage?

If you didn't rate yourself a 10, what can you use from this chapter to shift your mindset around cancellations?

_____

_____

_____

_____

_____

_____

_____

_____

_____

SUMMARY

As we can now see, Karen's pride in her lack of cancellations was misguided. Maybe if she were a customer service rep, it would have been a badge of honor, but as a salesperson, it was not. Turns out, she also had a low closing percentage because she didn't like "pushing" anyone to buy, so she typically waited for her prospects to tell her when they were ready. This meant she was missing a lot of opportunities where she should have used her selling skills to move more of the right people forward, despite their fear of change. She realized people whose fear couldn't let them remain clients would cancel, but in her heart of hearts, she knew it wasn't due to a lack of benefit to them. She shifted her focus to using Authentic Persuasion to lead more people to buy and stopped being afraid of those comfort zone cancels.

It seems very counterintuitive at first that I would advocate for a certain number of cancellations/returns and make a blanket declaration that if you have zero cancellations, you are failing as a salesperson. But as we saw, when you have zero cancellations, there is a good likelihood you are operating as an order taker. To be a sales professional, you must persuade a high percentage of your prospects to move forward. This will make some uncomfortable. They will feel uneasy about it, maybe during and after. They might even try to cancel or return what they bought if their fear creeps back in after the deal is closed.

Once again, remember this discussion of being a sales professional with cancellations is predicated on properly doing the prequalifying step with each prospect to determine if they are a good fit. You must go through the process of identifying them as someone who could be successful with your product or service, and then your role shifts to being a salesperson. At this point, using persuasion to move them forward is actually your duty. You literally fail them if you let them come up with excuses not to buy from you.

In the next chapter, I will talk about how to prevent cancellations. I know I just said you should have some, and even know which buyers will try to cancel. But, in the next chapter, I am going to cover how to prevent buyer's remorse so you can retain as many sales as possible and have very satisfied clients. At the end of the day, I don't actually want you to have lots of cancellations, so you must find the right balance in your conversations. This is really more about mindset and sales process than metrics.

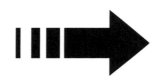

CHAPTER 18

PREVENTING BUYER'S REMORSE

*"You have to learn the rules of the game. And then
you have to play better than anyone else."*

— Albert Einstein

The first thing Steve did when he got to the office each morning was check his voicemail. He did it because it was important, but mostly, if he didn't, his boss would be upset when he found out Steve was avoiding customer calls. Steve hated the feeling of dread he had as he pressed the buttons to listen to his new messages. Most days, there was a voicemail from someone who had changed their mind after signing up with him recently, and now they wanted to cancel and get a refund. Next, Steve would log into his computer and check email; there was a good chance he would find messages from customers who had questions, were confused, or had changed their minds as well. Steve thought of himself as a good salesperson who did the right thing for the people he sold to. He was courteous. They all seemed to like him. He thought they trusted him. Yet he found himself starting many days behind—in the hole, sales-wise.

In the previous chapter, we looked at the Cancellation Paradox— as a sales professional you will have a certain number of cancellations, returns, or people who get close to the end of your sales process before bailing. Remember, the key here is using only acceptable principles of persuasion to move the right buyers forward. If you are twisting arms and manipulating buyers, the Cancellation Paradox doesn't apply to you.

While the Cancellation Paradox applies to most, this chapter is here to help you proactively prevent buyer's remorse. While some cancellations or returns are expected—after all, you're pulling your prospects out of their comfort zones and causing them to temporarily face down their fear of change—there are also important steps to take during your sales process to keep them at a minimum. My goal in this chapter is for you to proactively do everything you can to prevent prospects from waking up in the middle of the night, second-guessing their purchasing decisions, mentally spinning out of control, and leaving you that dreaded cancellation voicemail, sending that email, or walking back into your store or office first thing in the morning.

WHY IT HAPPENS

Buyer's remorse usually kicks in once the rush of emotional excitement and endorphins wears off. The positive feelings are replaced with feelings of doubt and/or regret. For most people, if the purchase price for something is relatively small, buyer's remorse is less likely. Usually, you won't feel bad if you buy a pack of gum and don't enjoy it. But you would probably feel buyer's remorse if you bought an expensive piece of jewelry and didn't like it even if you had researched it and picked it out specifically. While all buyer's remorse comes from a place of fear, the exact cause truly depends on the individual.

Some factors that lead to buyer's remorse include the buyer's past experiences, which will shape how they feel after the purchase. Have they made mistakes before that justified this behavior-specific fears? For example, if they bought something significant before (like a car), and it turned out to be a lemon, they could be way more cautious moving forward. This will be compounded if they had a parent who gave them an, "I told you so" speech after. If they got caught up in the excitement of the purchase, buyer's remorse could hit them like a ton of bricks afterwards.

The more skilled you are at persuading your qualified prospects to buy outside of their comfort zones, the more likely buyer's remorse could kick in afterward. They will constantly be looking for ways to backtrack on their perceived mistake before it's too late. On the other end of the spectrum, if the buyer is on a streak of good decisions, they will feel more confident and relaxed about their purchase, and if it was a mistake, there are still more wins than losses. Fundamentally, are they a glass-half-full or glass-half-empty type of person, and by extension, a buyer?

When will buyer's remorse hit? Everyone is different. Sometimes buyer's remorse hits a week later, sometimes the next day. I have even seen people literally call to cancel within minutes of signing up. Anything that happens too quickly after the sale is complete is certainly the direct result of a bad sales rep.

HOW TO PREVENT BUYER'S REMORSE

Let's talk about preventing buyer's remorse first. The optimal approach is to be proactive whenever possible. The best way to avoid buyer's remorse, altogether, is to move through your sales process, spending the necessary time at each stage, from rapport building to creating trust, asking questions, acting like a doctor to diagnose their situation, and assuming the solution. Knowing that buyer's remorse comes from fear, your goal is to take steps before the sale is completed to address the prospect's fears.

The question-asking phase has the most potential to help alleviate buyer's remorse. When done correctly, your questions will reveal deep insights into the prospect's goals, fears, struggles, and maybe even past pain or failures. Assuming that what you are selling actually helps the other person and addresses any (or multiple) of those categories you uncovered, the key is to constantly remind the prospect during the buying process of how this purchase will help their situation. For example, if you are selling credit repair services and you know the prospect's goal is to buy a home, then you want to weave in reminders of how the credit repair will help facilitate them in achieving that goal as you complete the enrollment.

When your solution addresses the prospect's specific situation, it should offset buyer's remorse. The bigger the prospect's why and the more strongly your product/service helps them accomplish or attain that why, the less chance of buyer's remorse. It is also important to use active listening when the prospect is asking questions to focus on where those questions are coming from. Most questions are signs of fear or concern. You want to ensure you follow the steps outlined in Chapter 9—listen, acknowledge, and address their questions completely.

Often, salespeople will answer prospects' questions, but at the same time, try to gloss over the answer or move on too quickly, usually out of their own fear of losing the sale. If the prospect asks you a question, do not hurry through the answer. That doesn't mean you should give long-winded answers (Remember—no dancing!). Your goal is to ensure they feel confident with your answer, and they are okay with moving forward. Giant red flags should go up if the prospect asks the same question more than once during your process. That signifies a really hot topic in their minds. If you downplay their concerns and get the sale, they will feel buyer's remorse. Using strategies like Empathetic Reversing will help.

HOW TO MITIGATE BUYER'S REMORSE

You have gone through your entire selling process and addressed everything possible—both the topics the prospect brought up and the ones you know most people have questions about. In my sales experience, I have always found the best approach is to be open, honest, upfront, and authentic. When you can anticipate what the prospect is thinking or might worry about, you will have amazing results in your sales career.

I always ended my sales interactions with my standard anti-buyer's remorse disclaimer: "One last thing. I have been doing this for a long time, and after we get done here, there will be a point where you will come up with questions you forgot to ask or concerns about how this all works. It might be at 2 a.m. that you wake up worried you made the wrong decision. That is totally normal, and I want you to know in advance that, based on everything you told me, you are making the right decision. But know that I am in this business long term—so you can call me tomorrow, or next week, or next month with whatever questions or concerns you have."

I tell each person that because I want them to be prepared for the panic they may feel that will wake them out of deep sleep. And when it happens, they will, hopefully, be relieved by reminding themselves, "He told me this would happen; now go back to sleep!" It is calming and confidence-building when you've told them something will happen and it does. And when it does, because they expected it, there is less surprise and fear around it. It is also powerful because sales reps who used manipulation tactics or left out important and unpleasant details would not make this type of statement. They hope their new client will lose their phone number.

This step is also vital when you know another party could influence your customer's decisions. If you are selling to one person and you know their spouse, parents, adult children, friend, boss, or business partner may be asking them questions that could potentially make them feel like they made a mistake, then make sure you mitigate that in advance. You might say something like, "Now, I know you mentioned your spouse would want to know more about this. Sometimes, it is tough for my clients to explain it to someone else. I talk about our program day in and day out, so if they have any questions or concerns, have them call me or the two of you can call together. Let me answer their questions and help them see how this will help the two of you with your goal of _____. I also recommend this because then your spouse can direct their concerns at me and not at you."

Once the sale is consummated, your buyer will start to hear that voice in their head debating the merits of their choice—like the angel on one shoulder and the devil on the other in a cartoon. Even though you warned them, it will still happen—the feelings of doubt and fear. Depending on what you are selling and your sales cycle, I also recommend salespeople make a post-sale follow-up call within the first twenty-four to forty-eight hours.

A follow-up call accomplishes two things. First, it will show them you are actually in the business long term. Again, ill-intentioned salespeople will close the deal and move on without ever looking back, usually from fear of giving the buyer a chance to return what they bought or cancel their service. But that is exactly what you want to do—show them you care about them. Remember always to do the opposite of what the slick salesperson would do. This will show them how different you truly are.

The second benefit of the post-sale follow-up call is to address those concerns that popped up in the buyer's mind. It could be questions they had but were afraid to ask during the sales process or worries that came up after the fact. You want to solidify everything possible so the buyer feels confident with their purchase. If those internal issues are left unchecked, they will fester and grow like an infection in a cut on your finger. While it might hurt a little and take some effort to address those concerns, you want to make sure you re-close your sale.

BUYER'S REMORSE EXERCISE

How would you rate your proactive process to help mitigate buyer's remorse for each new client?

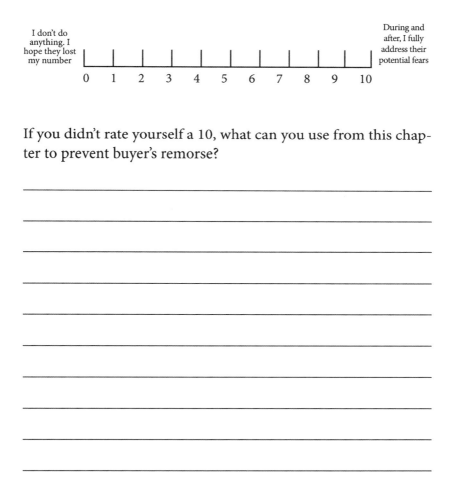

If you didn't rate yourself a 10, what can you use from this chapter to prevent buyer's remorse?

_____

_____

_____

_____

_____

_____

_____

_____

_____

_____

SUMMARY

Steve's cancel request voicemails and email were not because clients didn't like him; they happened because he was *too nice* during the sales process. Most people wouldn't think that was a reason for cancellations, but Steve came to understand that by shying away from asking questions, he was not going deeply enough with prospects to fully understand their biggest needs or concerns. Being honest about his sales performance, Steve saw there were also times when prospects asked questions and he didn't respond well enough to help them feel like they were making the right decisions. Turns out, since they liked him, they bought from him anyway, then changed their minds later. Steve shifted his approach and actually went deeper with his prospects while at the same time pushing the right people forward for their reasons and not his, and then he set the right expectations for how they might feel after. That's when he saw a significant drop in the unpleasant voicemails and emails. Soon, he came in each day excited to check his messages, mostly from happy clients thanking him. And any negative messages could be addressed, and he was okay if they happened because Steve knew he did everything possible during the sale.

Your goal should be for your customers to be happy and successful with what you sell them. Every person will experience some level of buyer's remorse after (and sometimes during) buying a product or service of value. Keep in mind that "value" is different for everyone; what might be inexpensive and goes unnoticed to one person could be a really big deal and expensive to another. To some, the decision to buy a $5,000 watch is nothing; to others, buying a $100 watch could create anxiety.

The best way to avoid the full effects of buyer's remorse is to complete each stage of your sales process, including active listening. Do not shy away from fully addressing the prospect's questions and concerns, or they will come back to haunt you later. Keep in mind that remorse is a fear response based on personality, tolerance for change, bad buying experiences, or what others have warned about, and how much they are influenced by people in their life.

If you are planning on a career as a long-term sales professional, always remember that the sale isn't closed once the transaction is done. You will find that, depending on what you are selling and the buyer's individual personality, you will have to follow up with the buyer and re-close the deal. Never forget that something will wake the buyer up in the middle of the night in a panic, so your job is to remind them that what you sold them was exactly what they needed and wanted.

And when they feel confident that they made the right decision, and see you as the hero who made it happen, they will be more likely to refer their friends and family, which we will cover in Chapter 20. But before we can talk about referrals, it's important we discuss a topic that defines a true sales professional and has the ability to empower order takers to fully embrace their mission to persuade.

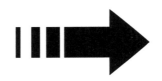

BEING HONEST BY SAYING NO

"Honesty is the best policy."

— Benjamin Franklin

Barbara had worried about getting into sales. Her biggest concern was having to talk people into buying even if they didn't want to. She had the impression, like most people, that to be a successful salesperson required manipulating and pushing, arm twisting and convincing. She knew people who bought things they really didn't need at the hands of a pushy salesperson. Her cousin had talked Barbara into taking a sales job with her, convincing her that she would be good at it, which was the only reason she was there. Once she was in sales, she found that not everyone she spoke with was a good fit to buy. She wanted to suggest a different solution instead of what she felt required to sell. She was constantly concerned that if she did that, her manager would get upset with her for not closing more deals even if someone didn't really need or want what she was selling.

On our journey to transform you from order taker to quota breaker, we have been creating rapport, building trust, and then assuming the close like a consultative doctor. Using questions is key for discovering if you are speaking with a qualified prospect. From there, remember, don't stop until they stop you.

What do you do when they aren't qualified? What if you are going through your process and uncover that they are not a good fit for what you sell? What if it turns out they actually don't want it? If you are in an industry where your product or service either solves a problem or need or helps someone get to a better situation (their goals), then you will soon discover that not everyone qualifies.

If you are in a sales position where "everyone wins"—where the expectation is that everyone you speak to should be sold to, then you can skip this chapter. But if there are some people who need or want what you have and others whom you can't help or who won't benefit, then this chapter is for you. If you are worried that sales success only comes from lose:win (they lose, you win), and that's part of why you hold yourself back while selling, this chapter is definitely for you.

WHY NO

First, we must address: Why would you ever tell someone no? Because they are not a qualified prospect. This might seem like an obvious statement, but I feel it's important to cover. If you have a product or service that solves a specific problem or satisfies a need, you will have prospects that it was meant to help and others who aren't the right fit. That second group, the unqualified prospects, are the ones you are telling no.

Now for the underlying reason—because it is the right thing to do. Doing the right thing is always the right thing to do. The challenge is that internal and external forces cause most salespeople to struggle with doing the right thing for their prospects 100 percent of the time. Whether it's the end of the month or quarter and you haven't hit your numbers yet, your company is having a contest and the top rep wins some big prize, or you are stressed about the bills you need to pay, many factors could sway your judgment.

If you are in the sales game with the goal of a long-term, professional career, the only way to operate is to treat your prospects differently than the "standard" sales mode. Now keep in mind, being in sales for a long time is different than being a profession-

al salesperson. There are life-long salespeople who use manipulation to get their way, who use sales as a vehicle for their ego,
who hunger for money, and who will do almost anything to get
paid. I have seen those long-time salespeople who are constantly
switching companies throughout their careers, as they hop to the
new, hot product or service with the biggest commissions, generally, at the expense of customers. Sometimes they have to switch
industries to run from the bad reputation they have created.

If you happen to be in that group, I hope this book can be the roadmap for seeing a different and very effective way to be successful in
sales. The world wants your selling power, just not the forcefulness
and manipulation. If you are not in that group or worried about being made to join that group, yet you want to be successful in sales
and sleep well at night, then it's all about always doing the right thing.

I am also talking to the order takers who didn't want to get into sales
in the first place because they thought being successful meant making each prospect buy no matter what. This is where I feel like your
power of empathy (as we covered in Chapter 11) is critical to what
the world needs, which is honesty in sales. But to leverage the power of empathy to push the right people forward or help the wrong
people go in a different direction is tough for most salespeople. The
order takers tend to let the prospect decide for or against. The hardcore salespeople always go for the sale. The key lies in knowing who
a good client for your company is actually and then taking action.

ABUNDANCE REVISITED

An interesting thing happens inside you when you are fully willing to tell an unqualified or uninterested prospect no. To me, it
truly means you are on the path to becoming a professional. More
of a consultant than a salesperson. Having a bag of "nos" in your
selling toolbox means you have made it to the place where you
are honestly looking out for the other person's best interest above

your own. You are operating from a place of abundance. The act of telling someone no in order to do the right thing for them means you realize there are more than enough opportunities out there, and you would rather sell to the people who would really benefit.

One caveat to this abundance mentality where there are "plenty of fish in the sea" is that you still have to do your best in each selling situation. A balance exists between telling someone no because they truly do not qualify or would not benefit, and giving up too easily because they are asking too many or increasingly difficult questions you aren't prepared for, or there are barriers keeping them from buying. The best way to determine how you are doing is to ask yourself, "If I didn't make the sale, could I say I did every-thing (the right things) I could to help that person buy?"

BENEFIT OF NO

Sometimes you saying *no* to an interested, yet unqualified prospect ends up being a gift you give that person. They say it's better to give than to receive, but most people like both—give a gift and get one in return. And telling some prospects *no* can sometimes be a better gift for yourself than trying to force that sale on the wrong person.

Imagine for a moment this scenario, which has happened to most adults: The check engine light goes on in your car, and you feel a sense of dread. Why do you feel anxious or worried when that light turns on? Because now you need to take your car to the mechanic or dealership, which could lead to an expensive repair. Since most people don't have the equipment to identify what's wrong with the car, they are at the mercy of the mechanic's diagnosis. The mechanic connects a scanner to your car's computer, runs the scan, sees there is no issue, and tells you your car is fine. They reset the system and send you on your way, without even charging you for the diagnostic scan.

After the shock wore off that what you were worried about (them charging you lots and taking advantage of your naivety) didn't happen, what would you do next? Most people would go tell everyone they could about their experience. And when asked "Do you know a good mechanic?" would immediately start evangelizing the shop they went to as the best, most honest shop around.

All because they told you *no*. Sure, you weren't hoping to buy something or spend money at the mechanic's shop, but you went there with a problem, expecting the worst (based on first-hand experience or stories you have heard), and maybe even with your guard up, feeling like you would have to defend yourself from an opportunistic mechanic. Yet that didn't happen. Instead, you found a professional who told you the truth while looking out for your best interest instead of their selfish interests. Sure, they could have talked you into some service you didn't really need, but they didn't.

My parents retired and moved from the San Francisco Bay area to a more rural area in California. After living there for a few years, they started hearing a clicking noise from their dishwasher. They got a recommendation for someone to fix it. He came out and after a few minutes determined there was a small part that needed replacing. Instead of selling it to them and charging for the service, he told my dad what part to buy and how to switch it out. Back in the Bay area, that rarely happened, and my mom appreciated it so much that she has since referred anyone who asks to him, resulting in more business and more income than he would have made charging them for something my dad could take care of.

The key when telling someone *no* is to leverage it into referrals. Like we will cover in Chapter 20, referrals are very powerful leads because the referred prospect already trusts you to a degree, and the wall of fear and hesitation is lower. If you want to receive the most powerful, open, and willing referrals ever, tell the wrong-fit prospects *no*, and then ask for referrals. I don't give a lot of sales "lines" to use in this book, but this is one to take, make your own, master, and use religiously. Start off with whatever is appropriate for your product/service and the situation: "There is nothing wrong with your car from what I can tell." "Your teeth look healthy; see you in six months." "Instead of paying me, get yourself some Drano and you should be good." Then roll right into, "I do a lot of business by referral, so if you know of anyone who needs a [your business], have them call me. I would love to try to help them out."

POWER OF NO

There is another benefit to telling people no: the power it gives me when I say *yes*.

Let me explain. As we saw in the previous section, several different types of no's exist. If you have a product or service that provides a solution to a certain issue and someone comes to you thinking they might have a matching problem or goal, and you discover you cannot truly or fully help them, then you would tell them no in a professional way.

Something amazing will happen in your mind, deep inside, consciously and subconsciously, when you become a professional salesperson who tells the wrong people no because when you tell someone yes (and work to persuade them using what we have covered in this book), you know you mean it. Even if they do not trust your efforts to close the deal are from the right place inside you, thinking you are just another salesperson trying to make a sale, you know the truth—that if you say *yes*, you really mean it; otherwise, you would have told them *no*.

At times, I have had prospects ask me the much-feared question, "Are you just trying to get me to buy *blank* so you can make money?" Knowing who I was and how I operated, I could confidently tell them my goal was to help them, and there were enough other people out there that I didn't need to convince them to buy anything, but that it seemed like they really needed what I was offering. I would also share with them the other recent times I told someone no who wasn't a good fit to help them realize I am not one of those "everyone wins" salespeople. The authenticity of my statement backed by the power of telling others no has always led to that conversation moving forward.

EXERCISING YOUR NO

Rate your effectiveness of telling the wrong prospects *no*, so you can tell the right ones *yes*.

If you didn't rate yourself a 10, what can you use from this chapter to ensure you are guiding each prospect down the correct path (for them)?

_____

_____

_____

_____

_____

_____

_____

_____

_____

SUMMARY

Barbara's biggest fear of being in sales was making everyone say yes. Sure, there would be people who would tell her no, but she felt pressure as a salesperson that her success was predicated on using any means necessary to make as many people buy as possible. The wild part is that she didn't even know where that pressure came from, other than her perception of what it meant to be a salesperson. Barbara's world and career changed when she discovered that to win long term at sales actually meant helping the right people buy and not forcing the wrong people to do anything. In fact, she started to enjoy the conversations with those who didn't qualify because she knew she was doing the right thing for them. This, in turn, made telling the right people yes and assuming the sale so much easier because she knew in her heart she was always doing the right thing for people. This helped her go from order taker mode, waiting for prospects to tell her what they wanted to do, to sales professional, taking charge to help each person get to a better place.

I know this might seem like the strangest chapter to find in a book about sales. On the surface, reps who let prospects walk away, or worse, tell them to go away, would be fired by most sales managers. But if an organization truly understands that not every person you speak with should "be a win" for the company because what you are offering isn't for everyone, then this is a very important chapter to embrace. I am not advocating telling random prospects *no*, but there is a power in telling those leads who are not interested or do not qualify that what you have is not for them. That power gives you amazing inner confidence when it is time to get the right people to *YES!*

Every opportunity you have with a prospect is precious. They have taken time out of their lives to speak with you about the product or service your company offers. In the event that the best thing for them, long term, is not to buy, make sure you leverage

that into a discussion about referrals. Always remember the mechanic story, and do not shy away from asking those *nos* for other
people they know whom you could help.

At the root of it, the key to saying no is an attitude of abundance.
If you know plenty of people are out there that you can serve and sell
to, you don't have to lose sleep over forcing the wrong people to buy.
Liz Lange, a pioneering fashion designer, says it perfectly: "Every
brand isn't for everybody, and everybody isn't for every brand."

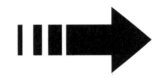

CHAPTER 20

GENERATING REFERRALS

"Always do your best. What you plant now, you will harvest later."

— Og Mandino

Victoria had great performance metrics. She had a good conversion percentage, did really well with inbound leads, and always exceeded her quota. There was no doubt on the sales floor that she had the skills to close deals. However, she didn't receive many referrals. It wasn't that her customers didn't like her or trust her enough to tell others about her. It was more that she didn't focus on generating referrals through her conversations or any post-sale follow-ups. Victoria was mostly focused on the sales she was trying to close today and not what she might get next month or next quarter. She had seen so many coworkers come and go that, frankly, she didn't even know if she would still be at this job in six or twelve months, so she didn't see the value in spending time building referrals.

A successful long-term sales career includes a balance of hunting and farming, similar to our ancient ancestors. Hunting is great (and usually necessary) when you need to eat today. Imagine you are a cave dweller waking up in the morning with the sunlight warming your body. Your belly is grumbling, and you know that as soon as your family wakes up, their bellies will be wanting food as well. Whatever you can find to eat that day, whether it's catching an animal or foraging for berries and nuts, is what will keep you going until tomorrow.

Now imagine you wake up, step outside of your cave, and go through your fields, plucking yummy bites from the bounty that has been planted, protected, nourished, and is now ready to eat. There are benefits and stresses to each. Neither is *the* perfect option. Hunting can lead to big kills that will feed a village, or to a lot of energy spent with nothing to show for it (after all, it's called *hunting*, not *catching*). Farming could create so much food that you will need to figure out how to store it, or a cold snap, bugs, or fungus could wipe it all out and leave you starving.

Our role in sales is much like the roles of our ancestors: to act as a hunter and think like a farmer. In this chapter, I want to examine what that means. For some in sales, this will be an interesting transition because, often, salespeople, especially when they are new and in "survival" mode, or only know one style, are mostly worried about their next deal, their next paycheck, their next meal. A hunter/farmer strategy requires both long-term thinking and short-term action. You want to play the long game when building your career, and at the same time, make it to see tomorrow.

HUNTING

What is hunting when it comes to sales? That is easy—the deals you can close now. Your primary goal each day is to close/sell/ enroll any deals that can be completed now. If you have the option to one-call close someone, do it.

Close what you can today. Don't assume anyone will ever call you back if they do not enroll today. In the car business, seasoned people joke with the new or less successful reps about the "Be-Back Bus" because, when you ask a new car sales rep about the prospect who just left the lot without buying a car, they will pretty much always say something like, "They really wanted to buy, but had to go. But don't worry; they will be back." When in hunting mode, assume that once the prospect is out of sight, you will never see or hear from them again. Short term, when in survival mode—so you can eat today—you have to allow some level of healthy urgency into your abundance mindset. Focus on seizing the most from opportunities, without becoming opportunistic. But at the same time, you have to be careful not to become desperate. Desperate salespeople can actually repel prospects—they can tell you are trying to get them to buy for your reasons, not theirs.

Act as if there is no "Be-Back Bus" bringing your prospects back to buy from you. Act as if you will never talk to that person again if they don't buy from you right now (again, whatever "buy" means in your industry, which could also mean various milestones along the way). Act as if not making the sale right then will keep you from paying your rent or mortgage or buying food. Act as if your life depends on that sale (while keeping in mind what we talked about in Chapter 11 about what your focus should be).

You will also have, as you have probably already experienced, a pipeline full of prospects who were not ready to buy right away for various reasons. It could have been a trust issue where they needed to do more research, a financial issue where they needed to find the money, or maybe a timing issue. Whatever their reason, make sure you are constantly working your pipeline. And keep yourself out of the Follow-Up Trap.

FARMING

Here is where the advice gets "complicated." In this moment, you need to act like a hunter, yet at the same time, think like a farmer. A farmer isn't working hard today so they can eat now; rather, they are planting seeds that will, hopefully, grow to provide food many months in the future. A lot of work is involved in farming. You have to get the ground ready, plant the seeds, water the area, protect the seedlings from predators and harsh conditions, and then gather up the bounty at the right time. The payoff for all that effort is a supply of food that will, hopefully, last for months or maybe even years.

The most important part of your farming sales strategy is planting seeds that turn into referrals. The key is long-term thinking about your sales career, like a farmer who stakes out a plot of land and commits to seeing their crop through to harvest. When you are selling products or services that require a consultative sales process, your process should yield referrals. The formula for maximizing referrals has two parts, as we'll explore in the next section.

GENERATING REFERRALS

Part One: The first step in maximizing referrals is exceeding the prospect's expectations. As Ken Blanchard wrote in *Raving Fans*, "Your customers are only satisfied because their expectations are so low and because no one else is doing better. Just having satisfied customers isn't good enough anymore. If you really want a booming business, you have to create Raving Fans." Mediocre experiences, ones that meet expectations but aren't really anything special, will not generate referrals.

That said, there will always be people who share their experiences. Even if the experience was just "okay," you might get some referrals, but that is not reliable. Bob Burg, author of the *Go-Giver* series, said, "All things being equal, people will do business with, and refer business to, those people they know, like, and trust." Remember, when the prospect enters your store or talks to you on the phone, they are expecting to go toe to toe with a self-centered salesperson who might try to use manipulation to make the sale. Once they realize you've broken that mold by approaching the sale in a completely different way through the use of Authentic Persuasion, and you solve their issue, need, or want, you will produce a *raving fan* who is excited to tell others about their experience.

Part Two: The second part of the referral-generating formula is—wait for it—ensure your prospects/clients know you appreciate referrals. As the saying goes, you won't get what you don't ask for—so ask for referrals. Brian Buffini, a long-time real estate agent, loan officer trainer, and coach, built his successful real estate business on telling everyone he wanted referrals. And what he teaches others (check out his books, podcasts, and live seminars if you want to generate more referrals) is to tell clients during each interaction that you want referrals. If you have done your job right and created a *raving fan*, you should have no hesitation in asking for referrals, and they should have no hesitation in telling others about you.

WHAT'S STOPPING YOU?

Many people in sales are not generating as many referrals as they could. The question is: What's stopping them? There are many possible factors, so if you are not receiving and closing a high percentage of referrals, it's important to assess whether any of these apply to you.

As I mentioned, the first one is salespeople don't ask for referrals. They don't bring it up during the sales interaction or in a follow-up. Maybe because they are only thinking short term. Or they already feel they have too many inbound leads to care about referrals.

Another reason is sometimes it is too early in the relationship to ask for referrals. This is valid because if the new customer hasn't used or experienced the product or service yet, it will seem weird to ask them to give you the names of other people who might also want it. Imagine going out to a nice restaurant, and as the host is seating you and handing you a menu, they ask if you know anyone else who would like to come eat there. You would think that absurd since you don't even know yet if it will be good enough to share.

Finally, salespeople might not ask or focus on generating referrals due to a lack of confidence. Sometimes they don't believe in themselves. Other times, they aren't aware of the true value thy have provided to their prospect. While I know it happens, there is also the scenario where the product/service isn't actually that good. If you went to a mediocre movie after eating at a mediocre restaurant, would you recommend either to other people?

It is important to understand what is stopping you from asking for and generating more referrals. Going back to where we started this book with self-awareness, if your referral-generating effectiveness is low, I hope you will spend some time uncovering why and then figure out solutions to overcome those mental hurdles.

REFERRAL EXERCISE

How well are you doing at actively generating referrals?

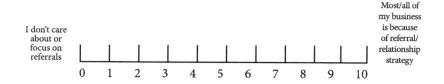

If you didn't rate yourself a 10, what can you use from this chapter to generate more referrals?

_____

_____

_____

_____

_____

_____

_____

_____

_____

_____

SUMMARY

Victoria had fallen into the trap that catches most salespeople—short-term thinking. It wasn't so much that she only wanted to hunt, but that she wasn't playing the long game with her sales career. Since she was thinking only of this pay period, she was closing deals (hunting) and not planting referrals seeds (farming). She didn't even know if she would still be in this position for very long, so in her mind it seemed pointless to spend any of her precious time following up with customers, asking for referrals, and nurturing relationships. If she had been our early ancestor, she might think she wouldn't even be "alive" long enough to harvest referrals, because, in her mind, winter was always coming, or that she would have to migrate to somewhere else, so it wasn't worth planting seeds.

At the beginning of this chapter, I said a true sales professional will be a balance of hunter and farmer, meaning they will close deals today while reaping the rewards of referrals. The ultimate goal would be to create a 100 percent referral-driven business. Now you might be thinking that lots of successful career salespeople just hunt and don't do any (or much) business from referrals. I would contend that such salespeople are not successful. To me, true success in sales, and in life, is freedom from the daily fear of where your next deal, or meal, is coming from. Success is not getting to the end of the pay period, or quarter, and having to scramble to make sales happen out of desperation. Success is having a system in place to help you achieve your goals. The type of salesperson who wakes up each day and must go hunt to eat is playing a dangerous game.

If your goal is to be a true sales professional, then you must do both: hunt and farm. I am not going to sit here and tell you that only referrals matter for the same reason it is a terrible idea to plant seeds, then sit back and wait for them to grow as your only food source. You must hunt/gather while you nurture your referral seeds. Since your time will be spent closing deals today, make sure you have a referral system in place to help nurture your clients and contacts in a productive way to yield future bounty. I would contend that the ultimate measure of your sales success will be the percentage of business you get from referrals. If you are not generating enough referrals, why not?

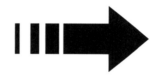

EXECUTING AS A SALES PROFESSIONAL

"Act as if what you do makes a difference. It does."

— William James

Maybe _____ has been in sales for years and wants to get their mojo back; maybe _____ is new to sales and wants to create success, or maybe _____ is contemplating a career in sales and they aren't sure if it's a good fit. _____ read a book about how to close more sales in a way that doesn't rely on closing tactics, slick lines, or manipulation. _____ made some interesting self-discoveries as a result of what they read and are now at the mental crossroads of putting it into action. _____ would love to have a life of success and freedom built around the irrevocable selling skills that any person can build.

This time, the starting story about a salesperson is *you*. Now that you have read this book, what is next? What will you do with this information? What short- and long-term goals do you have in place for your sales career, and how do the concepts from this book help you get there? To get different results, you have to take different actions and become a different version of who you are. What will need to change for you to use Authentic Persuasion to become a sales superstar?

My biggest goal and hope is that you put this information into action. As you went through this book, there were, hopefully, some concepts that caused a mental lightbulb to go off and inspired you to put something new in place. Please don't let this become another "shelf-help book" that you read, saw as somewhat useful, then let it collect dust, only later to pack it away, donate it, or sell it at a yard sale. This wasn't a work of fiction to read for entertainment—it was written to help you transform your sales career.

As you read through this book, you might have found many things that don't currently apply to you. I challenge you to reread this book in six months. That will give you time to apply the big lessons that hit the closest to home so they become awesome new habits. Plus, it will free you up for more concepts that weren't the most relevant the first time you read the book but could become important later, when you are ready. No matter what, apply anything and everything you found valuable.

Since I am all about taking action, I challenge you to do the same. On the ten lines below, I would love for you to write the ten strategies/tips/ideas/skills you learned from this book that you will put into regular rotation in your selling role in the next ninety days. Some people say it takes between twenty-one and thirty days to form a new habit, but since I don't like to half-ass things, let's focus on ninety days to make it super solid. What are ten different ways you will improve your sales effectiveness? (And in case ten seems like a lot, that is less than half the number of chapters in this book, so I gave you plenty to choose from! And you can look at your scores from the end of chapter ratings to identify which areas to start with.)

_____

_____

_____

_____

_____

_____

_____

_____

_____

_____

My publisher is mad at me, but I am putting another exercise section here. (I told you I am all about action!) On the lines below, I challenge you to set a sales-related goal. Without knowing the industry you are in, I cannot tell you exactly what goal to set. It could be a "number of units/deals" goal or a financial goal. It is one thing to write out different ways you can improve your selling process; it is another to set a goal. Your goal should follow the SMART goal guidelines (I always recommend Specific, Measurable, Attainable, Risky, Timeline), and the deadline should be no more than ninety days out.

_____

_____

_____

I know you might be avoiding writing your goal here. Maybe you think that since it's short term, you don't want it in here forever. But it's a great way to immortalize it. Then, when you read the book again in six months (and hopefully every six months), you can look back at where you were compared to your new point in the future, like little sales success time capsules.

Once your goal is in here, write it down on different pieces of paper you can stick on your monitor, tape to your bathroom mirror, put in your wallet/purse—everywhere and anywhere to help remind you daily of what you set. Having a goal will push you to use the techniques. It's one thing to buy a hammer and nails to put in your toolbox. It's another to use them for fulfilling your goal of crafting a piece of furniture, hanging a picture, or building a new home.

In this book, you learned how to tell whether you are an order taker or sales professional. We then took a journey together to build on your strengths, face your fears, and focus on *why* you are in sales. The key part that you hopefully picked up on was that salespeople are not just born that way—anyone can make themselves into a salesperson, especially with the idea of approaching sales in a way that actually benefits both you and your customers appeals to you.

You also learned that the more you focus on the questions you ask and the information you can uncover from your prospects, the more you can prescribe solutions like a doctor helping patients. I am also encouraged that you saw how having empathy for your prospects is necessary for long-term sales success.

I have been a part of many different sales organizations, selling different products and services, in person and over the phone. What you have read here is what I know works for me. I wrote this book because I have encountered countless people who, like myself, didn't feel they were "natural" salespeople and never thought they could be the person who used all the slick lines. I know if you apply even half of what is written in this book, you will outperform the sales reps around you.

When you shift your mental framework and your actions from being an order taker to using Authentic Persuasion, you will live a completely different life. Whether your goal is to make more income or to feel good about what you do for a living (or hopefully both!), I know you can use your strengths to help other people make purchasing decisions without relying on manipulations or tricks. The great part is I am not asking you to change who you are and be like anyone else. I want you to be you. When you embrace who you are, including the experiences and skills that make you unique, you will be successful in your sales career and in life.

Now that you have read my book, I would love to hear from you. I always enjoy talking to salespeople about what works and doesn't work for them, what challenges they face, and what new ideas could help them create more success. I also would love to hear what you found useful in this book, what didn't apply to you, what didn't make sense, and what is maybe missing that should be here. You can email me at jason@authenticpersuasion.com. Send me a message, and if there are any further ways I can help you succeed, I will do what I can.

I wish you only the best in your sales and life journey. I hope you always keep learning and growing so that you have more to give back to others. I wish you your own personal success, whatever success means to you. Enjoy selling with Authentic Persuasion!

Your friend,

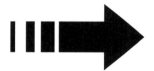

ABOUT THE AUTHOR

Jason Cutter didn't come from a sales family, but his winding journey led him to becoming an experienced sales success leader and consultant. The only child to a banker/finance manager mother and an engineer/program director father, he went to college at University California Santa Cruz and earned a degree in Marine Biology. After four years of tagging sharks and working in restaurants and two years at Microsoft on its technical support team, he finally got his first sales role at age twenty-seven.

Despite being a residential mortgage loan officer in 2002 during a hot real estate market, it wasn't until 2007 that Jason really learned the art of selling. Building a sales system and managing a team helped him understand and embrace his own selling style based on empathetic, problem-solving consultative sales instead of slick closing lines and manipulation.

Since then, Jason has led sales teams at multiple companies, some with over 100 sales reps spread across four offices in three countries. He has also worked with offshore call centers. His niche is really focused on inside sales teams that are also driven partially or completely by inbound performance marketing.

In 2017, he earned an MBA from Southern New Hampshire University, and now leads his own consulting firm, Cutter Consulting Group. Today Jason is supporting companies with sales success transformations of current groups and developing new teams from scratch. The mission of his daily podcast, *The Sales Experience Podcast*, is to change the way sales is viewed by prospects. *Selling With Authentic Persuasion: Transform from Order Taker to Quota Breaker* is his first book.

To learn how Jason can help you, visit him at www.JasonCutter.com.

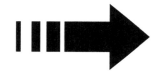

BOOK JASON CUTTER TO SPEAK AT YOUR NEXT EVENT

Are you looking for someone to educate, motivate, and inspire your sales team? Then Jason Cutter, the master of Authentic Persuasion, is just the speaker you need.

Jason Cutter understands the challenges business leaders and top performers face because he's been in their shoes. He spent twelve years working inside companies to create scalable sales processes that drove improvements in revenue and continued growth. Now as a consultant, he brings strategies, training, and systems to sales teams all over the world.

He has delivered sales motivation keynotes and conducted sales workshops in Europe, Latin America, and the United States. His presentations include original research and customized insight for each audience. He inspires audiences with practical insight, plenty of energy, and powerful, relevant stories that resonate long after the meeting ends.

By studying two concepts, connection and presence, Jason has been able to develop his fundamental teaching programs into what is today known as Authentic Persuasion, a program specializing in leveraging individuals' key experiences.

Jason speaks from a lifetime of accomplishments and first-hand experiences. He brings real-world advice, carefully researched facts, memorable humor, and powerful stories to the platform in order to wake up, shake up, and motivate audiences in ways that produce lasting results. He will offer strategies to motivate you and your team to action and improve your performance, relationships, and ability to think in new and creative ways.

Jason's passion for people is obvious and infectious. Jason will charm your audience and make them laugh, while they learn how to live the quality of life they dream about.

Jason is available to do workshops, presentations, and keynotes on the following topics:

- Using authentic persuasion
- Sales training
- Coaching versus managing
- Becoming a sales trainer
- Sales motivation
- Sales/revenue operations
- Sales success mindset
- Effective sales presentations
- Strategic selling strategies
- Collaboration between Sales and everyone else

To see a highlight video of Jason Cutter and find out whether he is available for your next meeting, visit his site at the address below. Then contact him by phone or email to schedule a complimentary pre-speech phone interview:

www.JasonCutter.com
jason@jasoncutter.com
Mobile: 206-234-1848